UNITED NATIONS CONFERENCE ON TRADE AND DEVELOPMENT

Social Infrastructure for Health: Guidance for social and consumer protection

United Nations

Geneva, 2023

UNCTAD/DITC/CLP/2023/3

ISBN: 978-92-1-113095-9
eISBN: 978-92-1-002590-4
Sales No. 23.II.D.7

ACKNOWLEDGEMENTS

This report was prepared under the overall guidance of Teresa Moreira, Head, and with the assistance of Pierre Horna, Legal Affairs Officer, Elizabeth Gachuiri, Economic Affairs Officer, and Zilu Zhou, Associate Economic Affairs Officer, of the Competition and Consumer Policies Branch, Division on International Trade and Commodities of UNCTAD. Robin Simpson, international consumer protection expert and UNCTAD consultant, drafted the report. Sophie Hunter and Elona Lazaj assisted the consultant and the team.

UNCTAD gratefully acknowledges the comments on drafts of the report received from the following: Claudia Cristina Robles Farias, United Nations Economic Commission for Latin America and the Caribbean; Housseynou Ba, Regional Office for Africa, Suvajee Good, Regional Office for Southeast Asia, and Tonia Rifaey, Regional Office for the Eastern Mediterranean, World Health Organization; and from outside the United Nations, Fran Bennett, Elizabeth Coll, Jonathon Lee and Claire Milne.

ACRONYMS

United Nations Agencies:

ILO: International Labour Organisation;

IOM: International Office for Migration;

UNHCR: United Nations High Commission for Refugees;

UNCTAD: United Nations Conference on Trade & Development;

United Nations Regional Economic Commissions (RECs):

ECA: Economic Commission for Africa;

ECLAC: Economic Commission for Latin America and the Caribbean;

ESCAP: Economic and Social Commission for Asia and the Pacific;

ESCWA: Economic and Social Commission for Western Asia;

World Health Organisation regional offices:

EMRO: Eastern Mediterranean regional office;

SEARO: South-East Asia regional office;

AFRO: Africa Regional Office

Other international organisations:

CARICOM: the Caribbean Community

ECOWAS: Economic Community of West African States

EEC: Eurasian Economic Commission;

MERCOSUR: Southern Common Market

OECD: Organisation for Economic Cooperation and Development

TABLE OF CONTENTS

FOREWORD

Origins of the programme: This paper was drafted within the component on Consumer protection and health services led by UNCTAD under the United Nations Development Account COVID-19-related technical cooperation project on *"Strengthening Social Protection for Pandemic Responses: Identifying the Vulnerable, Aiding Recovery and Building Resilience".* [1]

This project gathered the United Nations Regional Economic Commissions and UNCTAD to facilitate interregional cooperation and sharing of experiences in addressing the impact of COVID-19 and building resilient societies through social protection. [2] Consumer protection provided a significant contribution to two of the areas of social protection impacted by the COVID-19 pandemic related to the *strengthening of existing capacities and emerging gaps of core institutions responsible for the planning, design and implementation of social protections systems, in order to "build back better" as a response to the pandemic,* and to *building better knowledge and understanding about those in need of social protection, including the newly-exposed, leading to a more nuanced understanding of multi-dimensional poverty.*

UNCTAD has been entrusted by the United Nations General Assembly [3] the responsibility of assisting member States and other relevant stakeholders in the implementation of the revised United Nations Guidelines for Consumer Protection. [4] In addition, UNCTAD annually hosts the largest intergovernmental group of experts meeting on Consumer protection law and policy as the international forum for discussions, consultations and deliberations in this area.

The United Nations Guidelines for Consumer Protection refer to the connection between consumer protection and health within the consumers' legitimate needs (Guideline 5c), consumer education and information (Guideline 44) and within the recommendations relating to specific areas, on pharmaceuticals (Guideline 74), amongst other references. The UNCTAD publication "Achieving the Sustainable Development Goals through Consumer Protection"[5] first addressed both topics in a chapter dedicated to consumer protection in healthcare delivery (part IV). Within the aforementioned Development Account technical cooperation project, the Competition and Consumer Policies Branch of UNCTAD explored how consumer rights and the consumer protection policy could strengthen the provision of health services, contributing to enhance social protection system in the context of and in the aftermath of the COVID-19 pandemic.

Therefore, this component explores the scope for both operational and conceptual exchange, examining the potential for applying consumer protection principles to emerging developments such as eHealth and the concomitant concerns such as financial risk, digital exclusion, privacy and inclusion within health and other social protection services. The COVID-19 pandemic provided the spur and the context for this programme, which looks towards the evolution of post-COVID social protection, while seeking to improve it. The project has also widened perceptions of the possible range of health policy beyond the traditional Ministry of Health remit. [6]

This report follows the first report produced under this project on: *"Strengthening consumer protection in the provision of health services (including e-health) in the wake of the COVID-19 pandemic"* (2020). The recommendations of that report, set out in Annex 1, were very positively received during a series of regional webinars and through regional and national analysis and commentary, both written and oral.

Considering the scope of the technical cooperation project (Social Protection), in close cooperation with ESCWA colleagues, it was agreed that UNCTAD focuses on the recommendations of the initial report most relevant to build a 'Social Infrastructure for Health' (related to comprehensive protection in health; financing & affordability issues; eHealth, including identity & eligibility; and integration of informal sectors), therefore seeking a stronger connection to the core topic of the project.

Hence the choice of 'core' strategic issues emanating from five of the initial recommendations emphasising the need to develop, or maintain, ongoing structures for social protection.

The elaboration of the five 'core' issues has been carried out mainly through desk research, being complemented later by consultation with partners and member States' representatives. The presentation and discussion of this report confirmed the relevance of its recommendations.

SECTION 1. INTRODUCTION

At the UNCTAD 15 ministerial conference in Barbados in October 2021, the ministers of the least developed countries agreed a Declaration which coupled the immediate priority of *"recovery from the lingering COVID-19 crisis"* and the need *"to build and strengthen the bases to achieve sustainable and inclusive development over the medium term"*.[7] The Deputy Secretary General of the United Nations called for action to address gaps in infrastructure, including digital services, which this paper includes in the 'social infrastructure for health'.[8]

All the early general recommendations of the previous Phase 1 report (set out in Annex 1) are important for overall context. The selection of 'core' recommendations for this analysis was based on identifying where this project may be able to add value, within the time and resources available and it should not be taken to suggest greater merit on the part of any policy positions or indeed organisations.

The five recommendations which were selected for follow up form the core of this report. They include comprehensive protection in health, financing and affordability, ehealth, identity and eligibility and integration of informal sectors. These recommendations will be discussed in depth in section 2 below.

In sections 2 to 6 of this report, the key elements of the selected recommendations from the previous report are considered.[9] This leads to new recommendations set out in Section 7, which are still subject to further discussion.

This phase of the project aims to draw upon national examples, through the contributions from national jurisdictions, to identify problems, dilemmas, and good practice examples, acting as a 'reality check' around the feasibility of innovations. Such national experiences are drawn upon as much as possible using desk research, and bilateral discussions underway during the drafting process. it is hoped that they will result in further case studies from individual Member States.

This report addresses the infrastructure of services including the interface between healthcare services and financial support for their costs possibly extending to living costs when employment is interrupted, building on consumer rights. The report does not seek to address clinical matters. The report's wide scope duly considers the United Nations Agenda 2030 Sustainable Development Goals (SDGs), in particular SDG3: *"Ensure healthy lives and promote wellbeing for all at all ages"*.

SECTION 2. COMPREHENSIVE SOCIAL PROTECTION

2.1 COMPREHENSIVE PROTECTION IN HEALTH

The earlier report's recommendation on *Comprehensive protection in health* envisages social protection mechanisms related to health in three distinct regards.[10] The first two relate to the cost of medical services and income support for sick adults unable to work, as well as their dependants. SDG target 3.8 aims to: *"Achieve universal health coverage, including financial risk protection, access to quality essential health-care services and access to safe, effective, quality and affordable essential medicines and vaccines for all"*.[11] The International Labour Organisation (ILO) states quite clearly that: *"Social health protection has a twofold objective: universal access to affordable health care of adequate quality, and income security in case of sickness"*.[12]

Social protection systems covering access to health care (with associated costs) and related income support, have long been prominent in the OECD countries and have been emulated elsewhere, notably in Latin America and within public sector employment in many regions. This policy is designed for countries with stable employment patterns and public administrations that can take on the complex administration of benefits.[13]

Entitlement to social protection benefits may be through social insurance based on contributions by workers, (often matched by employers) or through social assistance based on proof of need (so requiring means test) reserved for people on low incomes and generally financed through taxation. Being based on current or recent income, or a proxy for income as a signifier of need, social assistance must steer between the twin risks of 'errors of exclusion', that is failing to reach those who are considered to need benefits, and 'errors of inclusion', that is extending benefits to those who are considered not to need them.[14] Benefits that are less selective in income terms are less prone to this problem.

Arrangements for health service financing and provision are diverse and not always comprehensive. For example, as discussed in sections 3 and 5, social insurance systems are having difficulty meeting the needs of large informal sectors and settlements. They are, nevertheless, contributing to social protection in terms of health care and of some cash benefits and are slowly increasing in prevalence, as became clear during the regional webinars.

Whatever system is established, the recognition of health as a human right in Article 12(1) of the United Nations International Covenant on Economic, Social and Cultural Rights which states: *"the right of everyone to the enjoyment of the highest attainable standard of physical and mental health"* implies a universal guarantee.[15] This concept of 'highest attainable standard' is spelt out in the preamble to the WHO constitution, which defines health as: *"a state of complete physical, mental and social well-being and not merely the absence of disease or infirmity"*.[16] This definition is both deep (*"complete"*) and wide (*"mental and social wellbeing"*) and these dimensions are reflected in this paper.

While promoting comprehensive provision, the ILO also stops short of advocating 'free' health services but enters two strong caveats: *"Out-of-pocket payments should not be a primary source to finance health care systems"* and that *"free prenatal and postnatal medical care for the most vulnerable should be considered"*.[17] The debate is vast, and cannot be resolved in this report. However, the report certainly notes in particular, the most serious issues of non-coverage and/or financial impoverishment resulting from costs of treatment.

SDG 1 aims to *"end poverty in all its forms everywhere"*. Its associated indicator 1.3.1 is: *'Proportion of population covered by social protection floors/ systems'*, going on to list various categories which include, among others, *'the poor and the vulnerable'*.[18] The SDG report for 2021 records that by 2020, only 47 per cent of the global population were effectively covered by at least one social protection cash benefit, leaving four billion people without a safety net.[19] Furthermore, coverage by at least one social protection benefit in high income countries was 85 per cent, compared to just over 13 per cent in low-income countries.

Estimates for health access specifically are even more difficult to assess as they raise questions of definition – in many jurisdictions, there is a general right to request basic health services but that is not necessarily reflected in actual service utilisation which frequently involves out of pocket payment. Nevertheless, the

2021 SDG report records improvements in coverage in all regions and in all income groups: the Universal Health Service Coverage Index increased from an average of 45 (out of 100) in 2000 to 66 in 2017. The most progress was recorded in Sub-Saharan Africa, the index rising from 23 to 44 over that period.[20]

This, however, raises the question as to precisely what is being measured here, for example, what does 'coverage' actually mean?   Coverage calculations used for SDG tracking include affordability and financial risk protection as well as a range of outcomes or 'proxy' indicators, such as blood pressure readings, which go wider than access, as noted with caution by WHO SEARO.[21]

These methodological complexities have serious implications for plans to extend eligibility for service to cover the entire population, for the calculations are geographical, social, and financial. This report notes the call by WHO for recurrent data collection as a major input in planning universal coverage and notes below in Section 3 the centrality attributed by WHO to 'out of pocket spending' by consumers in those estimates. [22]

2.2 PHYSICAL COMPREHENSIVENESS OF SERVICE

The notion of entitlement requires an infrastructure for ensuring delivery with adequate staffing to guide the users into making eligibility a reality. The provision of health services involves not only clinical functions but also administrative support, checking eligibility and patient records. This in turn requires a substantial, varied and dispersed physical 'infrastructure'.

The previous report noted the gradual 'normalisation' of eHealth, which is discussed below in Section 6. A WHO survey in 2016 noted how health workers accompanying patients in the community health centres could act as intermediaries in communicating with doctors at a distance, maximising the use of technology without placing the burden for its operation on the patient.[23] Being more dispersed, or even peripatetic, local community health centres may reduce transport costs for low-income users and raise uptake.

There are common sense limits to the dispersal of clinical functions where specialised equipment is required. However, one can conceive of administrative functions such as eligibility and enrolment in programmes such as vaccination becoming more dispersed with the use of electronic registers and

records. Help is likely to be needed in particular for initial registration, where new systems of eligibility are being rolled out electronically.

The widely quoted goal of universal health coverage does not just have to be about clinical treatment or on clinical premises. WHO SEARO make the point in correspondence that coverage is often discussed in terms of service utilization, rather than prevention of disease and promotion of health. They indicate that a major feature of Thailand's successful experience, for example, has been community health promotion funds that reduce health risks and 'catastrophic' health expenditure (see Annex 2) by promoting health throughout the life cycle, using community support systems. Local primary care facilities can be used as a base for such health education, which has the advantage of not requiring registration and so costs little in administrative terms. Other community networks may have a role to play, in taking such programmes to the people rather than requiring the people to come to medical facilities.

2.3 INCOME SUPPORT DURING PANDEMICS AND OTHER EMERGENCIES

The third element of the earlier report's recommendation on *Comprehensive protection in health* envisages *Income support during pandemics for those unable to work because of confinement and other analogous measures.* This came into prominence during the COVID pandemic. According to the SDG report of 2021: *"the COVID-19 crisis has demonstrated the importance of social protection systems to protect people's health, jobs, and incomes, as well as the consequences of high coverage gaps. During 2020 (after January), the Governments of 209 countries and territories announced more than 1,600 such measures in response to the crisis".* [24]

The SDG report notes that almost all (95 per cent, not including vaccination) of the social protection measures were short term. That should not be taken to mean that they have only limited significance in the longer term. The World Bank's 'living report' notes that the most widely adopted social insurance measures are waived or subsidized social security contributions (245 programmes), followed by unemployment benefits (172), and paid sick leave (134). Gentilini *et al* also reported 46 jurisdictions in which health insurance was provided as an emergency measure during the pandemic.[25] This suggests that the infrastructure of the existing social insurance systems can provide a useful framework, which can be extended in terms of both scope (the contingencies provided for) and coverage (the population covered).

However, where the scope of social insurance is limited, it may be necessary to inaugurate new systems. According to estimates from the United Nations Department of Economic & Social Affairs in March 2021, 82 per cent of social protection measures taken by the 51 member states of the African Union during 2020 in response to COVID-19 were not based on contribution records, while two-thirds of them introduced new programmes or benefits such as special allowances or grants, food and nutrition and health protection. [26]

At the global level, the 'living report' also found that most social protection measures (55 per cent) introduced during COVID-19 were provided as social assistance, (that is to say, not based on prior contributions) with the report finding that the poorer the country, the greater the usage of social assistance.[27] The most common instrument of social assistance is cash transfers and the report notes that: *"Only a minority of cash transfer programs are being scaled up based on existing schemes".* Indeed, 69 per cent were new and 29 per cent were 'one off' single interventions, of which few were universal, that is, without a test of means or of contributions. [28] This suggests that new systems are being devised but are still targeted in some way.

The second largest category of social assistance reported is support for, or postponement of, public utility obligations and other commitments, a simpler form of assistance which implies eventual repayment at a future date. [29] This is response to *'force majeure'* for consumer transactions is discussed in Annex 1 regarding the recommendation made in that regard in the earlier report. While such measures are outside the main social protection systems, they could use eligibility for social assistance to trigger such help. Consumer protection agencies could offer to act as brokers to negotiate and validate such schemes at scale, for example by drawing up model agreements for suspension of credit contracts or for eventual repayment of public utility bills. This could bring the different interests together to reach replicable agreements rather than swamp the courts or other bodies with unresolved issues. [30]

In summary, an important finding is that one of the advantages of social insurance is its relatively permanent nature, implicit in the concept of a contribution record. In contrast, social assistance mechanisms can be temporary and quickly established, often on a provisional basis.

2.4 INTEGRATION INTO SOCIAL PROTECTION SERVICES OF REFUGEES AND MIGRANT WORKERS

The earlier report's recommendation envisages long term development of systems for those social groups who currently lack coverage. Two clear examples are refugees and migrant workers, both brought into sharper focus during the COVID-19 pandemic.

2.4.1 Refugees: The United Nations SDG report for 2021 reports that *"At the end of 2020, about one per cent of the global population – 82.4 million people – had been forcibly displaced as a result of persecution, conflict or generalized violence"* [31] *Cross-border refugees are a far smaller number, around 26 million by 2020.*[32] *They are, by definition, removed from their abodes where they may have formal entitlement to social protection. Children make up around half of the world's refugee population and may lack any form of registration or identity as a result of their current circumstances. Obviously, this calls for rapid measures without strict conditionality.*

Under the New York Declaration for Refugees and Migrants, adopted in 2016 by the United Nations General Assembly, Member States made a commitment to: *"work to ensure that the basic health needs of refugee communities are met... We commit to providing host countries with support in this regard. We will also develop national strategies for the protection of refugees within the framework of national social protection systems, as appropriate".* [33] This last point links to current discussion around the need to 'mainstream' the treatment of migrants and refugees to bring them into line with national systems within their host countries and thus reduce social tensions (see below). Moves in this direction are reported in the West Asia region notably in Jordan and the Member states of the Gulf Cooperation Council. [34]

In some regions, concern is expressed among United Nations and WHO regional offices/delegates about the rising tension between host country populations and refugees, sometimes accompanied by a perception that refugees are being given preferential treatment.[35] Mandated by the World Health Assembly in 2019, the WHO is developing a global action plan to promote the health of refugees and migrants, their integration into the 'mainstream' and to counter misperceptions.[36] WHO regional office for South and South East Asia (SEARO) point out that the same problems can be encountered within jurisdictions by marginalised groups including indigenous people, populations of both remote areas and of informal peri-urban settlements lacking official recognition.

Some practical steps can be taken to address tensions that may arise when refugees receive cash for subsistence, which is not made available to host populations. Cash transactions may be a good way to help in their economic integration and there is evidence that refugees prefer cash to help in kind. [37] Some schemes (e.g., using pre-paid cash transfer cards) have been set up among refugee populations to facilitate cash transactions, which can help to 'normalise' refugee consumption patterns and reduce the need for data collection, thus raising fewer privacy issues and responding to fears of 'tracking'. [38]

Contrary to widespread impressions, not all refugees are in camps. Indeed, evidence gathered for the Turkish Red Crescent and the World Food Programme estimated that 84 per cent of Syrian refugee households in Turkey had at least one member in work, with only a small proportion actually living in camps. [39] Working inside the host community may well present a better prospect for integration than not working, while receiving health care. However, health care may only be available in designated locations, thus creating a dilemma.

Mental health: Matters are complicated further by particular needs among refugees for mental health treatment or therapy. A 2019 study found a 43 per cent prevalence of post-traumatic stress and 41 per cent depression among Syrian refugees in Turkey, a level ten times higher than among the host population. [40] Decisions in these circumstances are very difficult, but EMRO stress the 'utmost importance' of outreach to the refugee communities.

2.4.2 International cost-sharing: Obviously, refugees and migrants are not uniformly distributed around the globe and therefore neither is the disruption to the countries concerned. The 2020 report on migration and displacement for the G20 carried out by OECD, UNHCR and IOM, reported that, of the global refugee population of 26.3 million, the G20 countries, (which account for 80 per cent of global GDP and 64 per cent of population)[41], hosted only 7.6 million refugees (29 per cent). [42] 86 per cent of refugees are hosted in developing countries, 73 per cent in neighbouring countries and 68 per cent come from only five countries. [43]

Furthermore, the problems have been exacerbated by COVID-19. The G20 report found that *"resettlement, naturalisation and voluntary repatriation of refugees were all significantly reduced worldwide in the first half of 2020. With more people becoming displaced and fewer being able to return, resettle or naturalise, an increasing number find themselves in protracted and long-lasting displacement situations"*. The problems therefore are worsening, while the numbers displaced have continued to rise, for example in Afghanistan, Yemen, and Ukraine.

Leaving the cost of coping with refugees and other sudden influxes of migrant populations to fall on the receiving countries is economically inequitable and contributes to the tensions described above. Is there a mechanism for burden sharing? The United Nations Global Compact on Refugees in effect appeals for help from multiple potential stakeholders and sets out high level principles for aid to host countries, some of which deal with issues raised in this report, notably registration and identification. [44]

Could systematic mechanisms be developed for cost sharing, with a global centre of good practice as is being developed for migrants and is discussed in the next sub-section? Accurate registration and identification mechanisms could be used to implement simple funding formulae. The United Nations could perhaps play a role in negotiating the distribution of such funds from a global pool. The UNHCR Indicator 1.2.1 used to measure progress under the global compact is: *"Proportion of official development assistance (ODA) provided to, or for the benefit of, refugees and host communities, channelled to national actors in the refugee-hosting country"*. In the words of UNHCR: *"this indicator seeks to measure financial support provided to strengthen national and local institutional capacities, infrastructure and accommodation"*, with direct funding in support of the principle of 'localisation.' [45] A pooled fund would appear to be consistent with the New York Declaration of 2016, cited above, and indeed 'seed money' funding already exists on a small scale as well as emergency funds. These may contain formulae which might be adaptable.

2.4.3 Migrant workers and portability: There is category confusion in policy discussions in that refugees are sometimes lumped together with migrants,[46] who may be in a different category entirely when crossing frontiers voluntarily to work legally, frequently leaving families at home. They do, however, encounter problems of eligibility for social protection.

Agreements have been gradually negotiated on the 'portability' of social security rights across frontiers, often on a regional basis such as ECOWAS, CARICOM, MERCOSUR, and supranational European Union law. One common limitation is that they are usually based on social insurance mechanisms in their home countries. In consequence, they do little to help migrant workers in the informal sectors in countries of origin or of destination. Even for employment, which is formalised, receiving countries can be slow to ratify agreements fearing that their jurisdictions may lose more than they gain.[47] One noteworthy development at international level is that the African Union Commission (AUC) is currently developing a digital ID interoperability policy framework, which aims to enable people in Africa to obtain access to public and private services independently of their location."[48]

COVID may have temporarily changed things for the better in this regard as some (not all) jurisdictions have rapidly extended health cover to all residents in order to prevent infection. A more permanent arrangement is needed, but bilateral or multilateral social security arrangements are moving forward very slowly and in any case are far from universal in coverage as they tend to focus on retirement pensions rather than on benefits for workers. They can also be 'one way' only in that benefits may reflect only the contributions made in one jurisdiction rather than allowing accumulation of contributions made in both. This is wasteful and anti-consumer, in that contributions made go unrewarded.[49]

This issue is explicitly addressed by the United Nations Global Compact for Migration agreed in 2018, following on from the earlier (2016) New York Declaration for Refugees and Migrants already mentioned. Member States specifically made commitments to *"establish mechanisms for the portability of social security entitlements and earned benefits", and* further, to *"assist migrant workers to have access to social protection in countries of destination and profit from the portability of applicable social security entitlements and earned benefits in their countries of origin or when they decide to take up work in another country".* Accordingly, Member States committed to: *"conclude reciprocal bilateral, regional or multilateral social security agreements"* covering *"pensions, healthcare or other earned benefits"* and to *"integrate provisions on the portability of entitlements and earned benefits into national social security frameworks, designate focal points in countries of origin, transit and destination that facilitate portability requests from migrants".*[50]

The compact undertakes to *"establish a capacity-building mechanism in the UN, building upon existing initiatives, that supports efforts of Member States to implement the Global Compact"* including a *"connection hub that facilitates demand-driven, tailor-made, and integrated solutions. ensuring effective set-up for multi-agency and multi-stakeholder implementation"* going on to mention *"start-up fund for initial financing"* with *"seed-funding, where needed, to jump start a specific project.'"*

This is remarkable at several levels, including the degree of detail, the breadth of coverage across different forms of social protection and the pathway to possible multinational arrangements. It may reflect the widely noted political acceptability of social insurance and the notion of contributory rights, (rights which are much harder for refugees to exercise). It seems to recognise the possibility of an honest broker role for the United Nations or a linked body in making such cross-border agreements, and as such it raises the question as to the extent that such an agreement can be made for refugees too, as suggested in the previous sub-section.

COVID-19 has seen the balance shift towards inclusion of a wider range of groups. In this way, previously non-eligible populations, such as migrant workers or those working in the informal sector, have been included in public health services. The questions related to migrant workers and to refugees go beyond the customary scope of consumer protection. However, these groups do come within the remit of *'access to essential services'* as spelt out by the United Nations Guidelines for consumer protection as a *'legitimate need'.*[51] Furthermore, they may have accrued rights to service which they are not able to exercise in their current situation. The Guidelines refer to consumers *'regardless of nationality acting primarily for personal, family or household purposes.'*

SECTION 3. FINANCING AND AFFORDABILITY

The earlier report's recommendation on *Financing & Affordability* drew attention to the need *to mitigate the high levels of Out-of-Pocket Spending. (OOPS).* It also drew attention to the need for investment in public infrastructure services such as clean water, sanitation and clean energy which can bring the double benefit of improving public health while generating economic development. This second element is dealt with briefly drawing out an important link with the first, namely, the 'poor pay more' syndrome.

3.1 NETWORK SERVICES AND PUBLIC HEALTH

The utility infrastructure is not explored in detail here but discussed in the recently published UNCTAD paper on access to essential services. [52] The study emphasises the 'poor pay more' syndrome as a result of which, unit prices paid by non-connected consumers served by informal providers for water, sanitation and energy services are far higher than those charged to consumers connected to the official network. Furthermore, because of the poverty of the non-connected consumers, these amounts ended up accounting for 10 to 20 per cent of household income, even higher. Because these services have serious health implications, thus ranking among 'social determinants of health', there is a vicious circle at work. This syndrome has been widely observed including by UNCTAD in the Manual on Consumer Protection and successive World Bank studies. [53]

In their highly detailed multi-country study of urban poverty for the International Institute for Environment & Development, Mitlin and Satterthwaite traced the syndrome to health not only as a cause of ill-health as a result of *inadequate provision of public infrastructure and of basic services including health care,* but also in terms of higher prices for health services.[54] In doing so they regret the lack of data about health among the urban poor, partly due to the prevalence of national sample surveys which they say *"obscure the scale and nature of differentials within urban populations".*

In 2017 UNCTAD indicated the economic returns on investment in water and sanitation, including savings in public health.[55] Likewise, according to the World Bank president: *"The economic case for universal health coverage is strong. The Lancet Commission on Investing in Health looked at broader measures of growth and found that from 2000 to 2011 health* *investments were responsible for nearly a quarter of growth in developing countries".* [56]

3.2 NEED TO MITIGATE LEVELS OF OUT-OF-POCKET SPENDING, (OOPS) [57]

A WHO/World Bank report in 2021 on financial protection in health states clearly: *Out-of-pocket (OOP) health spending is an inefficient and inequitable way of financing health and should be reduced as much as possible in favour of pre-payment mechanisms.* [58] How is this to be achieved? According to an ILO brief in 2020: *"While several pathways lead to universal coverage, most countries reach it through mandatory schemes financed by taxes, social contributions, or a combination of both. The role of voluntary health insurance in health financing globally is small".*[59] However, for many people, the question is academic, because, remaining outside of structured health service eligibility, they must pay out of their own pockets, even though some services such as vaccination, may be provided free of charge through public health programmes.

The already mentioned recommendation on finance and affordability addresses the prevalence of OOPS, reported by WHO as around 40 per cent of total health spending in both low and lower-middle-income countries. [60] The ILO summarised in 2020: *"Each year, 100 million people are pushed into poverty because of expenses for medical care, while 800 million people spend at least 10 per cent of their household budgets on health care, with a particularly adverse impact on the poor"[61] The SDG report for 2020 reports that nearly 90 million people were pushed into extreme poverty by OOPS in 2015.* [62] The time lapse indicates the acute difficulty of accurate data gathering for this sensitive topic.

The above WHO/World Bank 2021 report underlines the importance of tracking OOPS: *"A full account of financial hardship requires monitoring of impoverishing health expenditures, including any amount spent on health out-of-pocket by the poor, in addition to large out-of-pocket health spending".[63]* The report points out that the SDG 3 indicator used to track 'catastrophic' and 'impoverishing' health spending draws upon measurement of OOPS. [64] The report then explicitly *goes one step further, to include a focus on the poor spending **any** amount on health OOP* (our emphasis).

The report goes on very firmly: *Those payments matter: they represent a major challenge to "End poverty in all its forms everywhere" (SDG 1) arising from OOP health spending by the poorest. Tracking all OOP health spending is critical to monitoring financial hardship across the whole population, in line with the pledge to leave no one behind that is at the heart of the SDGs.*

3.2.1 OOPS as index of coverage: OOPS is a direct measure of consumer expenditure. Given the recent emphasis on **any** expenditure on health by low-income households as indicated above, OOPS could be seen as a 'converse' indicator of the comprehensiveness of health services among poorer populations. Up to date gathering of data is therefore essential for planning. The 2021 report by the WHO and World Bank expressed concern that:" Immediate *actions are needed to improve the production speed and frequency of data on household OOPS and on total consumption expenditure. These adjustments are needed to reduce the current average lag of four years in generating indicators of financial hardship due to OOP health spending".* [65]

3.2.2 Trends in coverage: Given the presence of the financial element in the calculation of coverage, one might expect OOPS to fall as coverage rises, but this does not always happen quite so simply. In India, despite the coverage index rising from 50 in 2010 to 63 in 2020, OOPS levels remain high, at almost 63 per cent of current health spending in 2018. [66] This is despite the launch in 2008 of a non-contributory public insurance scheme to cover hospital care for people below the poverty line, further extended in 2018. [67] One possible explanation for the simultaneous improvement of coverage but only a modest decline in OOPS, may be that the poorer populations do not receive treatment to the extent of their entitlement or of their needs, thus resulting in continued OOPS.

Indonesia also saw an improvement in the index for health coverage, from 45 in 2010 to 62 in 2020, the largest increase in the region.[68] However, in contrast to India, OOPS fell from 48 per cent to 35 per cent of current health expenditure between 2009 and 2018.

Thailand's score in the service coverage index increased from 68 in 2010 to 82 in 2020. It is significant therefore that the lowest level of OOPS among the larger jurisdictions in SEA region is to be found in Thailand where the level of government funding is the highest (about two thirds of total current expenditure on health in 2018) even though external aid has virtually ceased. [69]

There is considerable scope for statistical confusion here, but are there patterns? WHO SEARO point out, *"Low public spending on health will either lead to a high share of OOPS, or high rates of foregone care, or both."* [70] Thailand's share of government spending is two thirds, Indonesia one third and India one quarter.[71] In 2015, Thailand had the fewest people impoverished because of OOPS, (listed as zero on one definition) which seems to support SEARO's thesis.[72] This is discussed in further detail in Annex 2.

3.2.3 OOPS and public finance: The WHO 2020 report on health finance found that the poorest countries often have the highest OOPS prevalence, reported as providing more than half of domestic health spending in two thirds of the 32 low income countries surveyed. [73] The report concludes categorically: *'If basic health care relies mainly on out-of-pocket spending, universal health coverage will not be reached.* [74] Furthermore, the use of donor finance has not reduced out-of-pocket spending as hoped. Rather, it has been found by WHO to displace public funding. This suggests a scenario in which the low-income countries can become trapped in a syndrome in which health spending is largely provided by foreign donors on the one hand and direct out of pocket payments by consumers on the other.

At a strategic level, this calls for consideration of the form taken by aid from donors and whether generic budget help, such as debt reduction, might be more likely to avoid the displacement effect described above. The debt reduction approach is suggested by WHO in the Southeast Asia region (SEARO).[75] In that region, healthcare coverage levels are rising and OOPS levels are falling, while aid flows have diminished and the proportion of government funding in health care funding is rising.[76]

This evolution may be difficult to emulate elsewhere, given the size of the shift that is required. In considering the annual expenditure required to reach the SDG targets applicable to universalising access to particular services by 2030, UNCTAD's report on the LDCs for 2021 indicates a need for an annual growth rate of over six per cent for health and 17 per cent for social protection.[77] This is a classic example of macro-economic difficulties having micro-economic consequences, namely OOPS.

3.3 MEDICINES AND OOPS

The above analysis suggests that OOPS will reduce if access to health services improves and that public finance may be a vital part of that process. A complementary approach to reducing OOPS is to find a way for prices to fall. The directness of the impact of OOPS on many of the poorest consumers merits closer scrutiny of its actual composition and the example used here is medicine prices. A WHO 2018 report found that governments pay only a small share, ten per cent, of the costs of medicines and medical supplies. [78]

Spending on medicines dominated OOPS in the Southeast Asian countries taking part in a WHO commissioned survey published in 2018. [79] The share of OOPS devoted to medicines exceeded 70 per cent in all but two countries. The only country in which the proportion was below 50 per cent was Sri Lanka, (albeit still amounting to one third) - a jurisdiction whose 'national formulary' in support of 'rational drug use' has been widely cited.[80] This concurs with a joint report by the WHO and World Bank in 2020, which recommended that: *"government should draft a national list of essential medical products to guide procurement. It could be based on the WHO list of essential medicines which is updated every two years."* [81]

The 2019 WHO report on health finance reported on variation in medicine spending across countries in the same income group, expressing the importance of both *"the way medicines are priced and the capacity of governments to implement specific cost-sharing policies."* [82] If, as in South and SE Asia, medicines account for a major proportion of OOPS expenditure then better control of medicine prices could have beneficial results for low-income patients. This remains the case even when there is reimbursement of medicine costs. The same WHO report shows that such refunds amount to only low single figure percentages in the primary health care sectors in low and lower middle-income countries, (but 19 per cent in upper middle-income countries). [83]

Generic substitution: The mitigation or reduction of medicine prices has been a major feature of health finance policy in the OECD jurisdictions, where there has been a significant evolution in the use of generic medicines. Generic substitution operates through prescribing by international non-proprietary name (INN) thus enabling the substituting of a medicine, with a lower-priced alternative medicine whether it is branded or unbranded generic. According to WHO Europe: *"This practice is in place in most European countries, predominantly on an indicative basis. In recent years an increasing number of countries have moved to make INN prescribing and generic substitution obligatory".* [84]

In the middle of the last decade, the highest proportion of public pharmaceutical expenditure was found in Germany (80 per cent). This is mirrored by Germany's high proportion of generic medicines in the pharmaceutical market, namely 82 per cent by volume, exceeded within the OECD only by the United Kingdom with 85 per cent. Strikingly, both countries have low values for the proportion by value, 35 per cent for Germany and 36 per cent for the United Kingdom. In contrast, neighbouring France with similar income levels had only 30 per cent by volume and 16 per cent by value. Such dramatic differences suggest a link with health finance policy, in particular the reduction of unit cost because of generic prescribing. New Zealand, which also practices a policy of promoting generics has similar proportions to Germany and the United Kingdom, 81 per cent and 34 per cent. [85]

The South and Southeast Asia study cited above cautions against setting expectations of such cost control measures too high: *"All eight countries have defined and regularly updated their essential medicines list and state their intention to provide medicines free-of-charge in public health-care facilities. However, other studies found that, for several reasons, most people in South-East Asian countries purchased medicines from private pharmacies, exposing themselves to higher risk of financial burden".* [86] This corresponds with the WHO/World Bank report mentioned above which warned that even when a policy of promoting generic products is adopted, these might still be sold at prices in excess of international reference prices, but to a lesser extent in public sector facilities. The pattern of medicines purchased by consumers from private pharmacies or other retailers where they have to pay the full price out of pocket, may thus further penalise those on low incomes. The loyalty of consumers to local retailers may also form a part of the explanation – strengthening the argument for local cooperation with consumer protection agencies.

Where drugs are dispensed on prescription by doctors operating inside health services, the impact of prices on consumers in mitigated. This is further evidence of the consequence of exclusion from entitlement to health service treatment, especially in view of the increasing emphasis, noted above, on the need to avoid any expenditure at all among the poorest households. If universal coverage is achieved and medicines are to be dispensed free of charge on prescription, then the burden of cost will be transferred to the budgets of the health services, possibly resulting in cutbacks in other areas of care. Reducing the price of medicines can therefore contribute to reducing the aggregate cost of the health service. Of course, it will not resolve the problems faced by consumers paying other medical costs or ancillary costs such as transport in an emergency. But it can make a contribution.

SECTION 4. IDENTITY & ELIGIBILITY

4.1 A RIGHT TO IDENTITY

The relevant recommendation in the previous report puts forward the principle that entitlement to a service should operate regardless of the form taken by the identity signifier and identification should be accompanied by appropriate data protection regulation protecting the consumer. The further evidence coming to light during desk research indicates that the issues are wider than identification, taking in also methods of application for service, in particular digital or otherwise. The previous report concluded that identity could become the key to eligibility both for clinical services and for non-clinical health-related services of a financial kind, such as income support payments where there is a clear need to monitor payments on a regular basis. This could be crucial for expansion of social registers, especially in low-income countries. [87]

SDG 16 *"Peace Justice and strong institutions"* lists as target 16.9 *"By 2030, provide legal identity for all, including birth registration".* [88] The relevant indicator listed in the SDGs is 16.9.1. *"Proportion of children under five whose births are registered with a civil authority"* Other tangible measures could doubtless be developed. Even the above apparently simple objective is far from achieved, the SDG 2020 report recording that *"One in four children continues to be deprived of legal identity through lack of birth registration, often limiting their ability to exercise rights in other areas".* [89] *Globally, only 62 per cent of countries had a death registration system that was at least 75 per cent complete in 2015–2019; under one fifth of sub-Saharan African countries reached even that level.* [90] *These problems may be compounded by the lack of postal addresses.* [91] If potential patients have neither electronic nor postal addresses, nor birth certificates (bearing in mind that date of birth may be used in identification) then outreach by services may be handicapped.

The distinction between identity and proof of identity shows up most clearly in gender differences in that women are generally less 'identified' than men, a difference of almost 10 per cent in sub-Saharan Africa. [92] In order to ensure non-discriminatory access, the fundamental fact of identity needs to be transformed into practical entitlement. The World Bank in 2020 set out the division of identification processes into 'identification' (who are you?) 'authentication' (are

you who you say you are?) and 'authorisation' (what services are you seeking?). [93] To this list one could add the question: are you eligible to receive such services?

Digital technology may help to 'enfranchise' potential users of public services hitherto excluded, given the potential for speed of individual registration (for coverage), for data recovery (for individual claims) and for collective aggregation/analysis (for public health surveillance). However, the nature of such innovations is that problems emerge during early usage and there is some evidence for that, discussed below.

4.2 SINGLE OR MULTIPLE IDS?

There is a somewhat technical debate about single or multiple identifiers. Sometimes a single identity is advanced as a right. [94] The single digital ID can appeal to administrators (fewer access points to record) and to consumers (fewer passwords and usernames to remember (or lose)). However, there are risks. For example, a single identifier for both identity and a wide range of public services would be a more valuable target for cyber-attacks than would a dispersed set of identifiers. [95]

A single database accessed by a single ID is also very difficult to maintain accurately if it is to go into further detail than the most basic information – name, date of birth, gender, nationality. The different aspects of our lives are subject to constant change, such as health treatment, education, employment, income. Each of those requires updating, and all updating processes carry the risk of error. Hence, a joint report on social protection by UNICEF and the World Bank pointed to the risk of *"excessive centralization"* which it found could *"lead to errors being propagated across programmes that have common points of entry, ... There may also be fewer checks and balances, as well as information asymmetries".* [96] The other side of the same coin is that the same report criticised *"fragmentation at the policy, programme and administrative levels"* characterised by *"high inclusion and exclusion errors, where those hardest to reach, the poorest and most excluded, are not covered".* Both criticisms can be correct indicating an intrinsic tension.

In her work for the ILO, Sepulveda points to the existence of two options for consumer access to benefits and services, one being the use of 'foundational'

ID systems, (often national IDs) and the other being 'functional' IDs, designed for particular services.[97] The two could be combined in a multi-step identification process, so that access to 'functional' health-related information could be subordinate to access to the initial generic 'foundational' ID.

Sometimes the greatest complexity revolves around the establishment of eligibility, for the answer to 'what services?' say, 'health' or 'income support', may be too broad. A given sector such as health, may need to be broken down still further as different databases could co-exist with differing degrees of sensitivity and thus protection. For example, children's vaccination records might already effectively be known to education and health authorities, if they are based on school-based inoculation programmes, while their parents' personal records could be highly sensitive.

Furthermore, much data is collected in variable 'units. For example, income support may be assessed on a household income basis, while health records will usually be individual. Such differentiations logically suggest separation of data into silos. Safeguards are needed so that using a 'foundational' ID to gain access to a 'functional' database (such as health records) does not lead to 'leakage' between databases of different services.

4.3 TECHNOLOGICAL NEUTRALITY AND ENTITLEMENT TO SERVICE

The recommendation of the previous report, cited above, concerning identity and eligibility spells out the principle of technological neutrality; that is the principle that a citizen's entitlement to a service exists irrespective of the means of verification, whether 'over the counter' in a public service office or clinic or online. Fears are growing that access is becoming 'digital by default', although some legal judgements have upheld the right of access.[98]

A recent report on electronic IDs in 10 African countries by the Centre for the Internet and Society of Research ICT Africa, raises this question, concluding that: *"while many systems purport to be digital, they are often much more analogue in practice"*. In addition, national reporters warned that adoption of digitisation as 'silver-bullet solutions', by policymakers, development agencies and development banks coupled with the *"uneasy marriage between paper and digital systems"* might lead to the neglect of offline inequalities, or even exacerbate them.[99] For practical reasons then, the report recommended that *"digital approaches to*

identity should always be accompanied by analogue options to avoid or mitigate exclusion risks.... ensuring that there are always alternatives if digital approaches do not work (e.g., due to a lack of electricity or Internet connectivity)."

A World Bank report published in 2020 points out that: *"many countries still use paper-based registration or application forms to collect data during the intake process, and then enter that data into computers".*[100] The same observations were made by the WHO eHealth Observatory in 2016.[101] The World Bank study lists commonly required documents, including:

* identification and residence information (for an individual or for all family members), such as ID credentials, marriage and birth certificates, or proof of residence.

* documentation pertaining to labour status (certificates from employment offices).

* income statements (from employers or the social security administration).

* certificates of disability, pregnancy, and other health status.

As noted earlier, such documents may not exist. If major exclusions are not to take place, governments and systems need to have policy in place about how to treat their absence, other than simply turning people away. Procedures may be temporarily short-circuited during emergencies such as COVID-19, but more permanent arrangements will need to be set up to deal with this common contingency.

Digital divide: Not building fail-safe approaches could be dangerous for reasons which are self-evident in cases of break down, such as internet or electricity failure or lack of documentation. However, there is a more subtle danger (not unlike the European Union policy concept of the 'digital divide') under which, as digital mechanisms become ever more prevalent, those left out become ever more isolated. This exclusion is not necessarily a matter of technical possibilities for access. As is discussed in Section 3 on eHealth, the lack of access is often due to cost of transmission or of devices. The International Telecommunications Union (ITU) has pointed out that of the 3.7 billion people who remain unconnected, 85 per cent are covered by a mobile broadband network. In those cases, it not internet coverage which is the issue.[102]

According to the African Union Commission, over four fifths of African countries are reported to have national

ID systems using electronic databases, and biometric data is collected in more than two thirds of African countries.[103] Yet those who do not have access to the internet are still numerous and vulnerable to the syndrome described by the Centre for Internet & Society which is that: *"many of the countries examined make access to certain government services dependent upon having access to identity, meaning that digital identity becomes mandatory or de facto mandatory, even if the lack thereof is not criminalised."*[104] *This is precisely the syndrome of which the first report warned.*

Flexible design for eligibility and identity: One can imagine a variety of arrangements of foundational and functional IDs varying also between one-step and multi-step processes with the case for one or other model varying through time, place, and service. For example, the case for two step processes becomes stronger once there is a comprehensive foundational ID in place. But this may be a long time arriving in remote regions or informal settlements, given the existing lack of basic birth and death registrations already mentioned. It would be perverse to deny people access to urgently needed health treatment for which they could supply the necessary data locally, because they do not have access to a national ID which may take time to arrive.

In the 'real' digital world, there are other such practical snags. For example, older electronic devices may be second hand and not updated as initial contracts lapse. This could result in people carrying insecure IDs or even lose access to them altogether. Such problems need to be forestalled by recognition of the continued validity of face to face or paper-based systems.

'Person centred': Many consumers have, in any case, a preference for dealing with a 'real person' in applying for eligibility for a service. Such cultural obstacles feature in a 2019 study of the application of 'digital inclusivity' into French social protection systems.[105] While digital systems have become very widespread, the study concluded that users of many services, two thirds in the case of retirement pensions, and 58 per cent for the health insurance card, (both well-established services), remained attached to paper-based administration. Over a wide range of service, a 'human relationship' was found to result in a sense of control and engagement with the relevant institution, even in a country such as France with a high level of digital usage. These feelings are sometimes based on

the practical experience of consumers being locked out of their own accounts, sometimes due to their own lack of IT knowledge, but also due to failings in the designs of the systems and problems of connectivity.

Such accounts are eloquently confirmed by the report in February 2022 of the French 'défenseur des droits', a public official charged with monitoring citizens' rights.[106] The report finds that the result of 'dematerialisation' of applications for public services is that: *"people show up, exhausted, sometimes desperate, expressing their relief at being able, finally, to speak to someone in the flesh… Dematerialisation, as conducted so far, is accompanied by a systemic passing onto the user of tasks and costs that had previously been the responsibility of the administration".* The report concludes that: *"Another approach is possible"* and advises administrations: *Give every user the choice of their method of relationship with the administration; do not trap the user in an exclusively digital relationship; Do not hold users liable for errors or malfunctions of public sites."*

4.4 PRIVACY AND ELIGIBILITY

It is sometimes argued that there is a trade-off between privacy and eligibility for services. A conclusion that could be drawn from the studies quoted is that in practice, where biometric identifiers are used for identification, then promoting eligibility 'trumps' privacy, with the encouragement of donor bodies for humanitarian reasons.[107] The same could be said of any surrendering of information to administrative authorities in order to obtain a service.

This is a classic example of two important principles potentially conflicting. It is important therefore not to see them as absolutes. The question, which may seem rather philosophical, is: to what extent can one respect one principle, without violating the other? It is interesting to note that in a recent survey by WHO Africa region, a suggested list of barriers to implementing health record systems in Africa did *not* list privacy.[108] A possible explanation may be an initial rush of gratitude when people receive a service for the first time without realising the problems that may arise in due course.

A further possible explanation for the lack of attention paid to privacy might be that ordinary consumers are not often asked the above questions. For example, a study of eHealth in Bangladesh found that privacy concerns of patients did not have a significant impact on provider concerns about eHealth use as it was only the providers who were asked about consumer concerns.[109] WHO Africa on the other hand has recorded anecdotally the stigma that can be associated with visits to health clinics during pandemics,[110] and there is a long history of people refusing to apply for social security allowances which are conditional on their proving that they are poor.[111] While ordinary consumers may not ponder the philosophy, they may well simply abstain from applying when it comes to giving up information.

Data minimization: Risk of accidental loss of entitlement can be reduced by a combination of dispersal of functional platforms and minimization of data collected. One 'zero data' model of digital ID is based on a third party verifying the consumer's credentials as opposed to providing a lot of data on many distinct aspects of the user's life. For example, an ID to buy alcohol may verify that the purchaser is 18 or over without having to show a date of birth. This 'ID verification' indicates entitlement to a benefit, without having to refer to, say, marital status, or income. This does not solve all the issues as there will always be some matters such as medical records, which are highly specific and necessary for treatment. But the 'zero data' model avoids one data store containing all of a person's life. There remains the problem of who holds the information that is verified, how secure it is, and how the data storage process is audited. This requires regulation.

This approach approximates 'data minimisation' as referred to in the European Union General Data Protection Regulation. Likewise, UNCTAD's data protection principles set out 'collection limitation' and 'use limitation'.[112] Research for the Tony Blair Institute puts forward the notion that *"Identity is about enabling a persistent relationship at variable levels of trust between multiple parties, which requires an ecosystem of different methods of authentication".*[113] The need is to *"design policy to enable persistent, trusted relationships with users, not to create one identity to rule them all".*

SECTION 5. INTEGRATION OF INFORMAL SECTOR WORKERS

5.1 INFORMALITY AND VULNERABILITY

The recommendation of the previous report dealing with *Integration of informal sector workers* calls for updating and expansion of social registers in order to bring the informal sectors into eligibility for social protection benefits including health care. This could mean using digital IDs with due privacy safeguards.

The term 'social register' has featured in discussion with partners with reference to the need for registration of individuals in the context of entitlement to social protection services such as social insurance and health services and thus to measures of coverage. While the COVID-19 crisis has witnessed improvised systems of protection, more permanent systems of entitlement are likely to require some kind of register of entitlement in order to maintain records of associated payments, such as health costs or sickness benefit.

Pooling to reduce vulnerability: As noted earlier, SDG 1 aims to *"End poverty in all its forms everywhere".* The linked SDG target 1.3 is to *"Implement nationally appropriate social protection systems and measures for all, including floors, and by 2030 achieve substantial coverage of the poor and the vulnerable."* [114] *Target 1.3 raises issues of definition as it can be argued that all those excluded from social protection mechanisms (estimated by more than one United Nations source at over 40 per cent of the world's population), are 'vulnerable'.* [115] *Vulnerability itself is a concept much debated, taking in risk of permanent and episodic conditions, not just actual eventualities. The ILO distinguishes between the explicit pooling of risk by social insurance and the individualised risk implicit in premium-based private insurance.* [116] *The WHO Health financing Guidance of 2016 describes the consequences of fragmentation of pools. It quotes the experience of South Africa where nearly one hundred separate voluntary schemes covered only 16 per cent of the population, while accounting for 44 per cent of total health spending.* [117] *This suggests that the 'vulnerable' become more so, when left in residual schemes because of individualised premium-based systems screening out the less vulnerable. The extension of social registers strongly supported by some United Nations RECs during the project therefore, in effect, supports general risk pooling.*

Informality: 'Informal' work should not be confused with 'casual' or intermittent work, for it may well be full time and regular. [118] It is characterised rather, by its non-registered nature and thus by its avoidance of such procedures as those related to tax and to social insurance contributions. Registration is necessary for any system linking work status and/or income to social protection. It may both set the parameters of entitlement and form the basis for remuneration of health service staff by capitation fees or item of service fees even if the user does not pay directly. It is needed for records to be kept of payments made either *by* the user (e.g., medical fees to clinics) or *to* the user (e.g., sickness benefit or subsistence allowance).

5.2 THE EXPANSION OF SOCIAL REGISTERS

The crucial question already raised is whether social registers are feasible where there are low levels of income and employment records. The webinars taking place within this project have indicated that the answer to that question is likely to vary by region. For example, ECLAC has pointed to "the urgency of consolidating universal, comprehensive and sustainable social protection systems", reporting that in the LAC region, before the crisis, only 47 per cent of economically active people contributed to pension systems. 77 per cent of employed people were affiliated or contributed to health systems. [119]

The 'glass half full' interpretation is that, while far from universal coverage, significant numbers of people are included within such systems. However, there is also a 'glass half empty' interpretation. The rise in coverage appears steady up to 2019. Between 2010 and 2019, in 12 countries in the ECLAC region, affiliation or contribution to health systems among workers aged 15+ rose from 68 per cent in 2010 to 77 per cent in 2019. However, ECLAC reports that such membership declined by seven percentage points in 2020, while coverage in the poorest decile was thirteen percentage points lower than in the highest decile. [120] It is not clear then, to what extent these trends could be taken to mean that the LAC region has already attained the target for *'substantial coverage of the poor and the vulnerable'.* The numbers are certainly not negligible, but the remaining non-included populations could prove the most difficult to register.

Nevertheless, there have been some remarkably rapid responses to the need to provide informal workers with emergency income support. One example comes from Togo, where five million workers in the informal sector received basic income payments during the COVID outbreak – registered by mobile telephone. [121] Thinking is needed on the extent to which such registration systems could be developed in non-emergency situations, bearing in mind the need to avoid the 'digital by default' scenario already described.

5.3 COVERAGE AND THE INFORMAL SECTORS

It has already been noted in Section 3.2.2 that the legal extension of coverage does not necessarily translate into actual utilisation, nor always into decline in OOPS. However, in Thailand OOPS has fallen sharply from the date of introduction of the universal care scheme in 2002, including the informal sector, thus suggesting that health coverage can exist outside of social insurance registration. OOPS fell from 33 to 18 per cent by 2008, below the comparable figure for the OECD countries at that time and decreased further from 16 per cent in 2009 to 11 per cent in 2018. [122]

5.3.1 Capitation fees: Thailand and Indonesia have recorded the most rapid increases of coverage in the Southeast Asia region's large economies and have also both seen declines in OOPS. It is notable that both use capitation-based systems of payment for outpatient care. [123] Capitation fees are fixed lump sum payments per patient paid to service providers for a given period. They can be used to provide incentives for health practices to register patients on an ongoing basis and can be adjusted for age, sex, and morbidity. They are sometimes criticised for encouraging medical practices to 'cram' as many patients as possible onto their registries and this can be countered by setting limits on list sizes. [124]

A WHO study of 'people centred' health services in 2015 found that reforms in funding arrangements had included the *development of capitation-based funding that pools resources from different sectors to promote intersectoral community-based care.* The 'sectors' listed included *health, social security, housing, immigration, urban development, and education.* The report concluded that: *there is growing evidence to support a mixed model of funding, in which the largest part is based on capitated funds, with the emphasis on pooling resources, but with an additional element of funding that supports payment for performance and innovation.* [125]

Such fees can be seen as the equivalent of 'availability payments' in other services as varied as electricity (stand by generators to meet peak demand) and toll-roads (to guarantee the continuity of the network even during periods of low traffic). They tend to be associated with primary care in recognition of its activities in monitoring and referral. Such systems can bring advantages in terms of continuity and accessibility and can also be a form of cost control.

The sheer diversity, illustrated above, of experience and variation in linkage of different elements of coverage makes it dangerous to generalize. One can however conclude that to the extent that extending health and other social protection registers is a way of increasing the risk pool, then that can lead to reduced risk of catastrophic and impoverishing OOPS, a risk which leads unknown numbers of potential service users to stay away. Research is needed on the different national relationships between improved service coverage taking in workers from the informal sectors, itself a complex calculation, and the financial burden on consumers. Some countries seem to have progressed on coverage while also reducing OOPS. The evidence presented here seems to suggest that extended eligibility sometimes translates into access but not always.

SECTION 6. THE DEVELOPMENT OF EHEALTH AND TELEMEDICINE

The recommendation of the previous report relating to eHealth strongly endorses its potential for improvement of health service coverage, especially in view of its acceleration during pandemic conditions and taking note of the caution expressed by the WHO and others, further elaborated below.

6.1 DEFINITIONS AND LIMITATIONS OF EHEALTH

Definitions: According to the World Health Assembly's resolution WHA 58.28 of 2005: *"eHealth is the cost-effective and secure use of Information & Communication Technology in support of health and health-related fields, including health-care services, health surveillance, health literacy, and health education, knowledge and research."* [126] *Semantic confusion abounds, between eHealth, mHealth, telehealth and telemedicine. eHealth is the most generic, as defined above, while mHealth is a subset using mobile devices and networks.* [127]

Telehealth and telemedicine may use mobile devices, but their key feature is identified by the WHO Global strategy on digital health for 2020-2025 [128] with its definition of telemedicine as: *"The delivery of health care services where distance is a critical factor.'* This does not necessarily mean that mobile devices are in use, although they may be, according to local conditions such as connectivity and bandwidth. What matters is the use of long-distance transmission, making possible the better use of clinicians' time and raising speed of diagnosis.

eHealth may not be as new as it sometimes appears. Simple communication by text messages for appointments has now become as routine as voice telephony, indeed in some ways it is preferable, as less disruptive, and perhaps more precise. Its use is hardly questioned. The Pan-American Health Organisation (PAHO), does well to remind us that most telecommunication services that work for health services are carried out on "non-smart" cell phones, include text messages for monitoring treatments, medication reminders, notifying pregnant women for check-ups, and other uses. [129]

Some electronic mechanisms have become 'normalised' within health services for communication and monitoring. Such functions have the great advantage for low-income regions of using widely available technology, including personal devices, i.e., mobile phones, whose take up has vastly exceeded expectations a generation ago. Such recent gains should not be taken for granted and need to be safeguarded.

To this end, it is important to remember that many recipients of messages will often be low-income households using devices that are obsolete or approaching obsolescence. Digital interfaces could be designed specifically for devices with low data storage, battery power or slow connectivity. These are helpful for consumers or businesses with less access to affordable devices, connectivity, and reliable energy supply. The name for this approach has been suggested as 'low intensity design' and could be used for example by people with second hand mobile phones. [130]

The range of innovation in eHealth is confirmed by a WHO survey of eHealth developments in 10 West African Member states ending in 2021. [131] The varied mechanisms included training field staff such as ancillary workers and midwives for basic diagnostics and public health reporting. Individual communications such as patient reminders for appointments featured as did logistical matters such as reporting pharmaceutical stocks. Maternal health was a particular feature and the late 2021 conference of the African Medical and Research Foundation (AMREF)received reports that self-monitoring data was collected on tablets (charged by solar power) operated, with great enthusiasm, by the mothers themselves. [132]

Limitations of legislation: The previous report's recommendation on eHealth identified the need for privacy and data protection legislation necessitating reviews of national privacy laws and sanctions, and appropriate institutions such as data protection authorities, as well as specific protections for health records and confidentiality.

Sepulveda reports for ILO that there is no shortage of legislation on privacy in many jurisdictions, but warns that it is not yet matched by effective application. [133] Furthermore, much privacy legislation and data protection has been developed for commercial use as ecommerce develops. [134] There may then be a need for review of data protection legislation from the specific health angle bearing in mind the far longer history of medical confidentiality, long preceding digital data processing in both the public and commercial sectors. [135]Consumer protection agencies may be able to help health services in this domain as is being proposed at the time of writing in the Philippines for platforms to be developed to warn consumers about marketing practices of health products. [136]

In a dramatic intervention, United States Federal Trade Commissioner Rebecca Slaughter has warned against placing too much faith in IT innovation in health, with reference to artificial intelligence (AI). She cites a study by Obermeyer *et al* in the United States regarding an algorithm intended to improve access to care for high-risk patients with chronic health problems. The algorithm was judged to have a racial bias originating in its use of care costs as a proxy for health needs. As white patients spent more on health care than black patients then this translated into the former being thought to have greater needs, effectively reducing the relative assessments of the latter. Commissioner Slaughter concludes that: *"Mounting evidence reveals that algorithmic decisions produce biased, discriminatory and unfair outcomes in a variety of high stakes economic spheres including health care."* She points out that *"the FTC has a body of enforcement experience from which we should draw".* [137]

This use of AI represents a more radical shift than simply speeding up data transfer as it impinges more directly on clinical decisions and health service management. Could such patterns amount to a kind of technological over-reach? Similar concerns, though more mundane, are expressed by WHO SEARO who warn of the limitations of mobile devices for health education and training given problems of continuity of connection and lower capacity to operate on the part of volunteers and ancillary staff who play an important role in health education.

6.2 MORE ACCESSIBLE INTERNET AND TELECOMMUNICATIONS ACCESS

Consumer protection and competition authorities may have experience of intervention in the electronic communications sectors, including price and access terms. The Pan-American Health Organisation (PAHO) makes links between health and consumer protection in communications regarding what is sometimes referred to as the 'inverse care law' by which *"those who need the most from the health system are those who have least access. In digital health this is amplified, as vulnerability of the population frequently*

accompanies the lack of connectivity. A non-equitable approach could end pushing vulnerable populations into even more precarious situations". [138] PAHO draws the distinction between mobile phone ownership and connectivity and warns against the *"false impression" that* all digital devices and their users could access health services remotely. *"When considering "access" to health services that can be provided via telemedicine, it is necessary to have smart phones and faster digital connectivity".* PAHO puts the rhetorical question: *"Is the Region of the Americas ready for the age of digital interdependence?"* It answers its own question very bluntly: *"Not yet. In fact, no region of the world is ready."*

The World Bank World Development Report 2021 spells out as follows the implications of the various technical shortfalls and their different salience in different regions: [139]

The **coverage gap** refers to the fact that 'last-mile' digital infrastructure has yet to reach all inhabited locations, so that, for technical reasons, a connection cannot be made in certain areas. The coverage gap varies from less than one per cent in North America to 29 per cent in sub-Saharan Africa, still very significant.

The **usage gap** refers to the fact that, even when coverage becomes available, uptake of the service by the affected population will typically not be universal. The World Bank reports that *"although the 3G coverage gap has shrunk by more than half over the last five years thanks to successful rollout of last-mile infrastructure, the usage gap has remained remarkably stable, indicating the persistence of barriers on the demand side".* So, the usage gap took in 42 per cent of the world's population in 2018, but 64 per cent in South Asia, where one billion people are covered by a broadband signal but do not make use of the internet.

Even those figures understate the problem, for household connectivity does not translate into household usage of all available services. So, to continue the World Bank analysis, the **consumption gap** refers to the fact that, even when people do take up the service, data consumption is typically too low to support basic economic and social functions, including some required for eHealth.

Confirming PAHO's warning about the cost of devices and connectivity, the ITU/UNESCO report notes that, despite the falling cost, *"nearly 2.5 billion people live in countries where the cost of the cheapest available smartphone is a quarter or more of the average monthly income…. Where extreme poverty persists, the affordability gap is even worse, with the median cost of an entry level Internet-enabled handset in Sub-Saharan Africa at more than 120 per cent of monthly income for the poorest 20 per cent of the population".* [140]

The obstacles set out above and below play out in different ways in different locations. For example, the 2020/21 UNCTAD evaluation of e-commerce readiness in Cote d'Ivoire is categorical in identifying internet access standing charges as an obstacle to digital development, especially when 35 per cent of the population lack access to electricity.[141] At a recent webinar/conference on eHealth in Senegal, organised by AMREF, a representative of the Senegalese Ministry of Health pointed to the 83 per cent telephone penetration and 30 per cent internet connection.[142] The difference between these two levels should give pause for thought, as should the widely reported differences between men and women in use of devices and thus internet access. This is particularly relevant to health services for children given the traditional responsibilities of women. According to research for the World Wide Web Foundation, men remain 21 per cent more likely to be online than women, rising to 52 per cent in the least developed countries. [143]

This raises global strategic issues that go far beyond the health and social protection sectors, while having a major bearing on them. The World Development Report for 2021 explains as follows: *'The high cost and low speed of internet services have emerged as key drivers of data consumption in the developing world. One reason is that many low-income countries lack their own domestic data infrastructure, relying instead on overseas facilities to exchange data (via internet exchange points), store data (at colocation data centres), and process data (on cloud platforms). This reliance requires them to transfer large volumes of data in and out of the country ("tromboning"), for which they pay a substantial penalty: prices that are several times higher than those in countries with their own infrastructure. They also experience slower speeds. This situation can be avoided by creating IXP* (internet exchange point) *infrastructure at the national level, eventually complemented by colocation data centres.* [144]

The concept of colocation could make a lot of economic sense in the social protection domain precisely because, it covers so many different sub-sectors, which could share costs while also requiring the same kinds of technical functions for storage and protection. Cost-sharing may extend to the use of the cloud, which has the effect of reducing redundancy by storing data on the internet, thus reducing the need to buy and manage data storage infrastructure. This creates options for a mixed system of single/multiple servers, connected, or not, to one another through the cloud. The possible permeations are too many to put forward a single model and the optimal choice of arrangement will vary by sector and subsector and population. However, if the cloud is built into data storage this does raise the question of jurisdiction over that data.[145] Public administration requires both confidentiality and access by national administrations. Other uses of the cloud such as financial services for refugees fearful of being traced, have found its extra-territorial nature to be an advantage. There are technical choices to be made which are policy matters, going wider than cost or efficiency of administration. The question here is: who regulates the cloud?

The development of IXPs can be expensive in the short term but such costs can be rapidly offset by savings in international bandwidth. The World Bank also reports that: *'By keeping data traffic in the country, IXPs can reduce reliance on international bandwidth, lowering costs and improving performance. One study covering Latin America noted that "local bits" are cheaper than "exported bits," finding that the region spent around US$2 billion a year for international bandwidth—a sum that could be reduced by one-third through greater use of IXPs'.* [146]

UNCTAD's Digital Economy Report 2021 points to the eightfold difference between average internet speeds between developed and least developed economies. [147] This has implications for the levels of use for patient treatment within pressurised services. It also has implications for the use of processed aggregate data for epidemiological purposes, to take an obvious example. [148]

It should go without saying that confidentiality of patient records should be respected but the issues go further than that. The WHO Africa region survey cited above, presents 'big data' as potentially beneficial and capable of: *"providing a powerful overview into trends and patterns in population health, to identifying individuals who are at risk from specific conditions. Further, big data is expected to help target early warning signs as well as enhance patient safety. Big data contributes to universal health coverage through the provision of new and unique data on populations and individuals that will support better health care for all".* [149]

Clearly there are major consumer protection and competition issues at stake here. It was discussed at the African online seminar, during Phase 2 of this project, whether the approach to be taken should one of focussing on access to e-services in general rather than e-health as a distinct issue so that tackling the generic issue would feed through to eHealth services in due course.

In South Africa, the generic approach was taken rather than specific measures for health services. Following a formal Inquiry into the cost of data by the Competition Commission, South Africa's dominant network operators announced that they would reduce data prices substantially from April 2020. The National Consumer Commission also conducted an informal Inquiry into data pricing practices of network providers. This resulted in the development of user subscriber regulations that compelled networks to carry over consumers' unused data allowances to the following billing period instead of automatic expiry. [150]

A further set of choices relate to the debate around regulation or competition to keep down prices. The World Bank in 2021, argued for keeping costs down through service competition at both wholesale and retail levels combined with infrastructure sharing to reduce costs. [151]

The consumer facing dimensions such as cost of device and of connection and service are relatively tangible and, up to a point, open to consumer pressure, but issues such as the above are beyond the scope of consumer choice and require other regulatory interventions. The same is true of the allocation of spectrum.

Spectrum scarcity: The boom in internet use worldwide has increased the value of the radio spectrum with considerable sums harvested by Member States through spectrum auctions. [152] This brings with it the danger that connectivity may slip backwards among the poorest. ITU/UNESCO report that *"2G and 3G services are now starting to be shut down in order to re-farm spectrum for 5G, and in some cases for 4G in emerging markets"*. The report warns that *"with formalization of the use of telehealth services, underserved communities and offline populations (such as seniors) are particularly at risk of becoming unable to access regular medical care unless issues of access are concurrently addressed, and issues of exclusion are mitigated."[153]*

As part of the *"checklist of actions and regulatory measures"* put forward by the ITU during 2021, one is *"address spectrum allocation"* in particular: *"support for fair and reasonable spectrum prices to ensure an adequate return on capital for licensees and thereby facilitate investment in capacity and new technologies, including 4G and 5G services"*. [154]

There is a risk that internet services and 2G phone services could be seen as in opposition to each other. Actually, each could benefit the other in its own way – positive experience of internet use will encourage other internet use. Existing connectivity, however modest, should be preserved during any drive towards more and better connectivity. There is widespread discussion of smart cities and *'villages intelligents'* (for example in Niger in West Africa) and community networks are developing also in Latin America, India, and Africa, extending beyond internet access to disseminating health information during the COVID-19 pandemic, proving content-related digital services on a communal basis.[155] Concessions to provide such communal services could be developed on the basis of 'negative auctions' as was done in Latin America and India in the early days of mobile phones. [156] There could be a public service obligation for internet capacity and certain key functions to be guaranteed at cost or on privileged terms to health services. Such obligations already exist for defence, especially for spectrum allocation, and may exist for other services.

6.3 EHEALTH IN A DECENTRALISED INFRASTRUCTURE

The pandemic has seen a huge increase in eHealth taking in the different functions spelt out in the World Health Assembly resolution quoted at the start of this section, that is to say going beyond clinical health care and taking in surveillance, (including self-surveillance) and health education.[157] It is also highly likely that some change in practice will be permanent, for example consultation at a distance, although, when done by telephone, this is hardly a technological revolution, but rather an acceptance that not all communications between clinicians and patients have to be face to face.

Some consider that public investment in health infrastructure is too concentrated around large-scale hospitals, sometimes at the expense of local community facilities.[158] eHealth and other e-services may enable a more flexible option for the development of networks of health centres (and not only centres focused on health) with facilities for consultation by internet in conjunction with other social protection services, thus enabling 'one stop' service. This is a development suggested by the WHO 2015 study of 'people centred services' already cited, based on *'intersectoral community-based care'.* [159]

The 5,000 *cybercentres* envisaged in Cote d'Ivoire, would aim to form a national multiservice network performing the function of service and communications centre allowing people to pick up both electronic messages and administrative documents such as birth and death certificates, a vital function in regions with few postal addresses. [160] One should bear in mind also the level of illiteracy (53 per cent) and the limitations that places on the involvement of patients unsupported to use the technology. The Philippines Ministry of Health are working to develop a satellite-enabled telemedicine GIDA programme to serve Geographically Isolated Disadvantaged Areas. [161]

These developments favour the development of multi-purpose centres that would require technological guidance to patients and doctors to be provided by health personnel other than doctors, whose time is very rationed and who may indeed be physically stationed elsewhere. Specialist support staff could be trained in both the ICT dimension (which could extend to patient record keeping and communication) and administration of health procedures such as testing and result reporting. Crucially, health workers accompanying patients could act as intermediaries in communicating with doctors at distance. The

WHO Africa region survey attaches considerable importance to the training of health staff regarding ICT skills *"A well trained and committed body of health workers is fundamental to providing quality and accessible services to communities and therefore a pillar of universal health coverage".* [162] Learning about how to perform a role in guiding patients through the technological processes of registration and monitoring could form a part of that training.

This would allow for a more localised service and be consistent with the strategic objective set out by the WHO strategy as *"people-centred health systems that are enabled by digital health".*[163] The buzz-phrase 'people centred' is widely used in current discussions without always being clarified. To the extent that it allows for health services to be personalised and localised, eHealth could facilitate the triangular relationship between health workers, clinicians and patients as discussed earlier.

The rapidity of consumer adaptability to technology, notably in Africa, suggests that non-take up of internet services is due not primarily to conservatism nor technological illiteracy but rather to cost as discussed above. People vary in their reactions and in the discussions around internet-based health functions, there is a danger of ignoring the progress that has already (and only recently) been made. The earlier analysis around comprehensiveness and the role of primary care suggests that there is potential for a health care infrastructure which is less centralised than hitherto. By facilitating consultation at distance eHealth could play a vital role in that regard.

SECTION 7. CONCLUSIONS & RECOMMENDATIONS

This section presents findings **with associated recommendations in bold italics**. Given the geographical diversity of the evidence, recommendations are flexible, and it is hoped that they can be developed further at national or regional level in consultation with partners and member States. Previous recommendations not considered here, remain valid. In this report, *Social Infrastructure for Health,* they have been identified by title only.

7.1 COMPREHENSIVE SOCIAL PROTECTION

(with reference to section 2 above)

7.1.1 Comprehensive protection in health: *Governments should set up national plans to achieve progressively universal coverage and effective access in health care, including the necessary financial support.* This is implicit in the SDGs 1 and 3, which emphasise respectively social protection floors and protection against financial risks for households. [164]

Given that the very significant variations in prevalence of the different systems suggest that there is no single template for universal coverage, there is a need for a guaranteed social protection coverage in default of other schemes.

7.1.2 Physical comprehensiveness of healthcare and social protection services: In aiming at full geographical coverage, ***governments should consider whether health networks should be less focused on hospitals as service hubs***. Digital systems operating from decentralised community centres, health centres or mobile clinics, could help in this process by speeding up the initial registrations for health and other social protection systems and subsequently improving communications between clinicians, health workers and patients. ***Help and advice with registration for social protection services such as income replacement benefits might be made available from community centres providing a range of services, not necessarily restricted to health.***

7.1.3 Income support during pandemics and other emergencies: Some of the responses to the emergency were remarkably speedy and effective, particularly when it came to income replacement. [165] Continued social protection measures may be required for some time to come, even in 'normal' times. During COVID-19, social assistance measures took in informal workers in some jurisdictions. ***Social protection measures introduced during COVID-19 may need to be maintained after the pandemic. If they are to become more permanent, they will require systematically expanding the various forms of social registers.*** Social insurance mechanisms are more suitable for the longer term but can be adapted for the shorter term (such as emergencies). Social assistance measures can be paid in cash or kind and on a more provisional basis.

7.1.4: integration of refugees and migrant workers into social protection services.

Refugees: *Consideration should be given to host country health services being compensated by an international cost sharing scheme to treat refugee populations, with the funding coming from United Nations member states on a pooled basis.* Such funds could be monitored and distributed by an international agency reporting to or a part of the UNHCR/WHO and in accordance with the United Nations General Assembly New York Declaration for Refugees and Migrants 2016. [166]

Migrant workers: International agreements on portability of social protection entitlements, while welcome as far as they go, are slow to develop and do particularly little to help informal workers migrating abroad. ***COVID-19 has shown that public health requires that migrant workers be entitled to basic health care in the country of destination based on a simple registration, rather than on membership of public or private insurance systems. Regarding wider social insurance rights, Member States should give consideration to requesting that an international (or regional) agency assume responsibility for brokering international agreements on cross-border portability of social insurance rights, initially based on the United Nations Global Compact on Migration.*** [167]

Governments should actively engage patient/consumer groups, or if they do not exist, should establish such machinery. Health and consumer protection authorities may collaborate to promote public awareness and participation, upholding people's right to information including about social protection. This was discussed in the previous report and may be the focus of future empirical studies.

7.2 FINANCING AND AFFORDABILITY

(with reference to Section 3)

7.2.1 Network services and public health. This is discussed in the recently published **UNCTAD** study: *Access by consumers to essential services, energy, water and sanitation.* (United Nations 2022), which identifies the 'poor pay more' syndrome under which the lowest income consumers pay the highest unit prices for essential services (water, energy, see Section 3.1 above).   This handicaps the health of inhabitants of non-connected areas, such as peri-urban informal settlements and remote rural areas. There is a risk that such a syndrome could exist in health services too, penalising those who are not registered with formal health services.[168] This has implications for the following discussion of out-of-pocket spending on health.

7.2.2 Need to mitigate levels of Out-of-pocket spending (OOPS): *Governments should closely monitor out-of-pocket consumer spending on health and its corollary: unmet need for treatment because of potential patients staying away from health services for fear of financial consequences.* These patterns are difficult to measure, especially when they require both consumer income and expenditure to be tracked. *Given the complexity of current indices of coverage and recorded patterns of health spending (or non-spending due to unaffordability), the relatively simple measurement of OOPS incurred by households seeking healthcare may act as a measure of restricted coverage by health services.* This report endorses the call by WHO and World Bank for governments to act: *to improve the production speed and frequency of data on household OOPS and on total consumption expenditure.* [169]

As a first step towards avoiding the worst consequences of OOPS and unaffordability of health care, ILO's recommendation 202 in effect prioritises avoidance of OOPS especially for prenatal and postnatal care. [170] *Governments should consider setting ILO recommendation 202 as the baseline for 'retreating' from OOPS. In due course a more comprehensive approach will be needed, requiring study of those countries in which this has been achieved.*

OOPS and public finance: Without 'domestic' government funding, low-income countries run the risk

of being stuck in a syndrome in which health funding is dominated by OOPS and donor funding, with very small proportions taken up by domestic government funding and social insurance. OOPS then becomes the default option as does non-treatment. *Member States should consider WHO evidence which suggests that donor funding should be redeployed to support government revenues through debt reduction or through appropriate technology transfers or capital programmes (such as internet exchange points for example) rather than become an integral part of health service funding.* Examples have been brought to the attention of the project from SE Asia, (see Section 3.2.2 above) of jurisdictions that have raised the proportion of government funding in health care, raising coverage, and reducing OOPS while aid flows have diminished.

7.2.3 OOPS and medicines: Medicines form a high proportion of OOPS incurred by many consumers in low-income countries. There also appears to be a pattern of generic substitution that reduces medicine costs in some high-income countries, particularly benefiting those patients who obtain medicines on prescription. *Given the prevalence of medicines in OOPS, the mitigation of pharmaceutical prices should be pursued through generic substitution supported by approved lists and reference prices. Public health authorities acting as primary payer for medicines should leverage their bargaining power to negotiate lower prices.*

7.3 IDENTITY & ELIGIBILITY

(with reference to Section 4)

7.3.1 The right to legal identity: The provision of a legal identity for all is an SDG target and its absence (which is widespread) can lead to people missing important public services. *Given the necessity for identification mechanisms to underpin the extension of eligibility for social protection, national governments need to address the underlying problem of lack of legal identity mechanisms, (such as birth registration) as recognised by SDG 16.* This is a problem which predates digital development.

7.3.2 Single or multiple IDs? A single ID providing access to the full range of social protection services may not be achievable because of the range and complexity of services covered. Furthermore, it could also be undesirable, because a single trove of data is more attractive to organisations carrying out cyber-attacks than is a dispersed set of databases.

The concept of 'foundational' (basic identity) and 'functional' (service specific) IDs has been discussed by the ILO and others in relation to access to social protection. Use of the 'foundational' national ID to prove basic identity is attractive in theory, but reliance on that mechanism as the general entry point for all public services can bring risks of exclusion for those billions of people with incomplete identity proof such as lack of birth certificates or addresses. The wider the application of a single foundational ID, the more serious the consequences of exclusion.

Dispersal of functional platforms (in conjunction with data minimisation) should be considered to reduce the risk of comprehensive loss of entitlement by individual consumers due to technical problems. Many consumers will be able to deal with the different sub-systems once they have been duly registered with the different services, but they will often need help in making that initial registration. This is an argument for local centres, (perhaps including mobile units), with internet capacity, having trained specialists operating under strict ethical codes to facilitate such access mechanisms.

7.3.3 Technological neutrality and entitlement to service: There are limits to reliance on digital systems given the problems of connectivity, affordability, and incomplete records of such basic data as registered births. ***Paper-based systems need to be maintained to the necessary standard, together with the element of face-to-face contact. These elements must be recognised and planned in from the start of any programme of innovation.*** This report restates the principle expressed in Recommendation 8 of the Phase 1 report that the technical mechanisms discussed above should not limit the underlying right to public services. ***Entitlement to access to public service should not depend on a single medium of application such as digital registration. The human right to health, including health care, should always remain in place and not be overridden by technical obstacles.***

7.3.4 Privacy and eligibility: ***Governments should enact and/or revisit data protection and privacy laws and verify their adequacy in the light of emerging collection, use, and sharing of digital data in the provision of health and other social protection services.*** Consumer protection agencies should actively advocate for upholding patient's rights to privacy and control over their personal data. Health authorities should clarify the scope of telemedicine and regulate qualifications and licensing, making sure that patient's rights will not be compromised.

7.4 INTEGRATION OF INFORMAL SECTOR WORKERS

(with reference to Section 5)

7.4.1 The expansion of social registers: There is copious evidence to confirm the continued large-scale exclusion from social protection mechanisms of people working and living in the informal sectors and zones. There is also some evidence that the COVID-19 pandemic has dented some of those exclusions as health and social security benefits were made available more widely with fewer conditions than hitherto. ***Governments should formulate plans to extend coverage for informal workers and to do so in a more permanent manner than the recent emergency arrangements.***

7.4.2 Prepayment funding and risk pooling: Note should be taken of the WHO's warnings that mandatory prepayment needs to be prioritised. [171] ***In the light of the principles of equity and solidarity, the poorest should bear the lowest burden, alongside the actuarial principle that risk should be spread across a broad population to mitigate adverse financial outcomes for individuals.***[172] One practical way in which social insurance eligibility might be built up for example would be for care of children and/or other dependents, such as the elderly or people with disabilities, requiring care to be 'valorized' and rewarded with at least a contribution record as if it were paid work. While this goes beyond the task of extending social protection to informal workers, such steps could increase eligibility among informal workers and their dependents without requiring complex earnings records.

7.4.3 Coverage and the informal sectors: Actual take up of services by consumers seems to be reflected in a decline in the prevalence of OOPS alongside increased public funding. Some remuneration systems for medical services encourage the 'recruitment' of patients by developing government funded capitation fees triggered by patient registration. This can represent a form of consumer choice, especially in urban areas. ***Governments should consider the use of capitation fees as a way of encouraging medical practices to recruit patients, thus improving their focus on the needs of consumers for access and availability.***

Sometimes increasing coverage has not been matched by reductions in OOPS. This raises the question as to whether widening consumer eligibility is matched by increasing uptake of services. If many of those potentially eligible to receive services such as health and social assistance do not enrol, this creates gaps between eligibility and actual take-up. *Governments should assess knowledge and administrative barriers to enrolment in public programs including those identified in digital processes. Streamlined application processes, multiple entries for enrolment, and user-friendly and accessible convenient electronic means should be explored to make enrolment simple, quick, accessible, and inclusive.*

7.5 THE DEVELOPMENT OF EHEALTH AND TELEMEDICINE

(with reference to Section 6)

7.5.1 More accessible internet access: In discussions around telemedicine in particular and eHealth in general, it is easy to forget that many innovations require costly devices and connections to 4G and 5G networks. These are either not available to many poorer regions or only available at very high cost. The result is that billions of people are covered by broadband networks but are not connected to them and, when connected, they cannot afford the more sophisticated services. As the 4G and 5G networks roll out there are reports that they are competing for spectrum with the 3G networks that do serve people on low income and could in due course crowd them out.

Renegotiating spectrum allocation will not be simple during the life of existing licenses and transitional arrangements may be needed to help customers to move to new networks or at least to ensure that existing groups of customers are not squeezed out. Such arrangements will need to include both airtime pricing and replacement handsets.

There are three potential recommendations which follow from the above:

- Competition authorities and consumer protection agencies in close collaboration with national regulatory authorities or other bodies responsible for communication services, should work together to enable the necessary internet services to be financially accessible.

This may be achieved through a combination of legislation and regulation and competition and consumer protection law enforcement, namely promoting increased market access of new service providers, implementing regulatory measures vis-à-vis incumbent service providers, intervening against anticompetitive practices and/or abuses of market power of dominant players as well as against unfair commercial practices in the market.

- Spectrum allocations should guarantee the continued availability of low-cost networks such as 3G.

- Governments should consider awarding concession contracts with public service obligations attached to encourage the provision of internet services on favourable terms.

7.5.2 eHealth in a decentralised infrastructure: The availability of internet connections is essential for decentralised health networks as discussed above. Such facilities could be used for health consultations face to face or at distance. *Patients should be supported throughout registration procedures should that prove necessary.*

7.5.3 Last word: Running through this report, including Section 6 on eHealth, there has been the theme of data as a public good.

- *Governments should strengthen their data infrastructure and their capacity to use data to inform evidence-based policy making and improve social health protection programmes.*

- *Governments should explore using public administrative data for research purposes to generate public knowledge towards the improvement of social health protection, ensuring data privacy and security. Governments should leverage social registries and public administrative data to identify new beneficiaries, increasing the inclusiveness of social health protection programmes. Governments should improve health statistics.* This will require confidentiality laws and protocols to be observed and consumers to be reassured on that score. Regarding the protection of health records, the traditional conventions need to be applied in the new context. The technology changes but the ethical framework does not.

ANNEX 1. RECOMMENDATIONS FROM THE REPORT ON STRENGTHENING CONSUMER PROTECTION IN THE PROVISION OF HEALTH SERVICES [173]

Recommendation 1- Human rights.

The right to health being recognized by the United Nations as a human right, Member States should consider the United Nations Guidelines for Consumer Protection, in particular using the 'legitimate needs' of consumers, as a checklist for the provision of health services.

The scope of consumer protection should be clarified as extending to all goods and services, (including those which are publicly provided) without excluding individual sectors. Sectoral legislation would apply but would not avoid consumer rights.

Recommendation 2 - Comprehensive protection in health.

Comprehensive social protection health service mechanisms are needed in three distinct regards:

- The cost of medical treatment through the cycle of prevention, diagnosis, and prescription (all or any of which may be free of charge at the point of use);

- Income support for sick adults unable to work, as well as dependants;

- Income support during pandemics for those unable to work because of confinement and other analogous measures.

Systemic development is required on a long-term basis for those social groups who currently lack coverage concerning the first two measures. The third measure applies to the current and future emergencies.

Recommendation 3 - Financing & affordability.

Systems are urgently needed to mitigate the high levels of Out-of-Pocket Spending, which have a very regressive effect. The development of such systems could be mandated to sectoral regulators (see Rec 4). Large scale public health interventions with low unit costs should be carried out to strengthen resistance to disease and thus mitigate costs of treatment for both the service and for consumers paying directly. Investment in public infrastructure services such as clean water, sanitation and clean energy can provide a double benefit of improving public health while generating economic development.

Recommendation 4 - Health services regulation.

Governments should confer the close oversight and monitoring of health services delivery to expert and independent regulators entrusted with the mandate to protect consumers/users' rights including looking into possible improvements. These regulatory bodies should be also conferred a mediation role (as Ombudsmen) and be encouraged to adopt a high public profile being able to deal with individual and collective complaints including those involving independent practitioners working within the health service. The governance structure of these regulators should include the participation of consumers/users of health services representatives in advisory bodies and in any wide consultation mechanisms, providing opinions and suggestions towards the increased protection of consumers/users' rights.

Recommendation 5 - Consumer grievances.

The treatment of medical accidents would benefit from less focus on liability of individual parties. Redress for injured consumers could be applied through more generic and administrative modes than the adversarial liability route, while systemic problems can be approached through less judicial procedures. Malpractice, where it occurs, can be dealt with by internal systems, through administrative or professional mechanisms, without obliging users of the service to trigger such proceedings. Competent consumer associations or other competent representatives of health-services users should be enabled to take legal action to assert their rights as, or on behalf of, users or potential users of a service.

Recommendation 6 - Consumer protection law enforcement and international cooperation.

6A - Enforcement of consumer protection: Consumer protection agencies need to maintain their vigilance in monitoring abusive business practices in the field of retail health-related products. They should also closely monitor the increasing sales of medical products online. Consultation with relevant international bodies should further enable cross-border investigations of abusive practices, should that prove necessary.

6B - Cooperation for Research & Development: (R&D) In the light of the urgency of research cooperation to help develop vaccines and other health treatment products, the scope for encouraging open-source research should be explored by consumer protection and competition authorities, in collaboration with health authorities, bearing in mind the need for investment in R & D and the lack of such research capacity in many low-income countries. Long term risks for competition need to be monitored.

Recommendation 7 - eHealth.

The development of eHealth is very beneficial especially in pandemic conditions following the approach taken by the WHO. Regarding privacy and data protection in health, legislation needs to incorporate both horizontal and vertical aspects, reviewing national privacy laws, with appropriate remedies for breaches and appropriate institutional safeguards such as data protection authorities, as well as specific protections for health records and confidentiality.

Recommendation 8 - Identity & eligibility

Consumers should be entitled to access to a service and equivalent treatment during service regardless of the whether their identity signifier is digital or other, with appropriate regulation to protect the consumer, adopting core international principles of data protection.

Recommendation 9 - Integration of informal sector workers.

Entitlements to health services and direct income transfers need to be remodelled so as to bring the informal sectors into eligibility. Social registers could be updated and expanded using digital IDs, with due privacy safeguards.

Recommendation 10 – *Force majeure.*

In the exceptional circumstances of the pandemic outbreak, an explicit declaration of 'force majeure' by governments, duly noted by courts and regulators, would recognize, and encourage the block renegotiations of consumer contracts. Statutory safeguards could be developed to limit arbitrary impositions and set down requirements for review.

ANNEX 2. MEASUREMENT OF COVERAGE OF HEALTH SERVICES AND OUT OF POCKET SPENDING

Sustainable Development Goal (SDG) target 3.8 is: "Achieve universal health coverage, including financial risk protection, access to quality essential health-care services and access to safe, effective, quality and affordable essential medicines and vaccines for all." This rolls up matters of physical access, quality, and affordability. The WHO Global Health Observatory explains that the specific targets 3.8.1 "coverage of essential health services", and 3.8.2 which gauges impacts on family finances, should be monitored together. The coverage index is a 'unitless scale' ranging from 0 to 100, (not a percentage) and is a 'geometric mean' of 14 tracer indicators including components of service coverage such as reproduction and maternal, infectious diseases, NCDs and service capacity and access. As WHO SEARO notes, the tracer indicators such as blood pressure levels and smoking prevalence, include some "that are not directly about health service access" but are rather: "proxy indicators, which should not be interpreted directly as percentage of population with access to essential health services."

The SDG financial indicator 3.8.2 contains more than one element, subdividing into "share of population at risk of catastrophic expenditure when surgical care is required", (defined as 10 per cent or more of income), and "share of people at risk of falling into poverty if payment for surgical care is required" (impoverishment). To illustrate the severity of risks, in 2020 in the Democratic Republic of Congo (DRC) and in Niger, 74 per cent of the population were at risk of catastrophic expenditure and 84 per cent of the people of DRC and 72 per cent of Niger were at risk of impoverishment. Unfortunately, a rather simpler calculation, that of the share of the population spending more than 25 per cent of household income on health is scarcely available. The difficulty of measuring catastrophic and impoverishing spending is that it requires collecting two sets of data – consumer incomes and consumer expenditure.

Out of Pocket Spending on health services (OOPS): OOPS is reported as percentages of health spending rather than proportions of household spending and there is a clear pattern that poorer countries tend to have higher OOPS. However, a weakness in OOPS for analysis of consumer detriment is that it does not trace the pattern of potential users staying away from medical services for fear of incurring charges. When that happens, the pattern may be even worse than that revealed by high percentages of OOPS. One possible way to capture some of the exclusion is to measure OOPS incurred by households that seek treatment.

Given the presence of the financial element in target 3.8 above, one might expect OOPS to fall as coverage rises, but this does not always happen quite so simply. The South and Southeast Asia region is particularly interesting in this regard because of the huge variation in OOPS ranging from 10 to 74 per cent of current health expenditure with an estimated 47 per cent for the region as a whole.

In India despite the coverage index rising from 50 in 2010 to 63 in 2020, OOPS levels remained high, at almost 63 per cent of current health spending in 2018. This is despite the launch in 2008 of the Rashtriya Swasthya Bima Yojana (RSBY), a non-contributory public insurance scheme to cover hospital care for people below the poverty line and vulnerable people. One possible explanation for the simultaneous improvement of coverage but only a modest decline in OOPS, may be that the poorer populations do not receive treatment to the extent of their entitlement. 'Coverage' may not always result in actual use.

Indonesia also saw an improvement in the index for health coverage, from 45 in 2010 to 62 in 2020, the largest increase in the region. However, in contrast to India, OOPS fell from 48 per cent to 35 per cent of current health expenditure (to a little over half the level in India) between 2009 and 2018.

WHO SEARO attributes the improvement in coverage in Indonesia, in part at least, to the merging of existing government health schemes in 2014 into the National Health Insurance Programme (JKN). By the end of 2019, the JKN had 222 million members (83 per cent of the population), including 96 million poor people. It may also help that social health insurance in Indonesia is also significantly higher than in India, the highest in the SEA region at 13 per cent of current health expenditure, more than doubling since 2009.

One, perhaps explanatory, difference between the major schemes in India and Indonesia is that, unlike India's RSBY as introduced in 2008, JKN Indonesia covers outpatient and inpatient care from the primary level up to the tertiary hospital level.

Thailand's score in the service coverage index increased from 68 in 2010 to 82 in 2020. It is significant therefore that the lowest level of OOPS among the larger jurisdictions in SEA region is to be found in Thailand where the level of government funding is the highest (about two thirds of total current expenditure on health in 2018) and external aid has virtually ceased. OOPS has fallen sharply from the date of introduction of the universal care scheme in 2002, including the informal sector, thus indicating that health coverage can exist outside of social insurance registration. OOPS fell from 33 to 18 per cent by 2008, below the comparable figure for the OECD countries at that time and decreased further from 16 per cent in 2009 to 11 per cent in 2018. The patient is free to register with recognised service providers in return for free treatment. The main source of finance is government expenditure, (almost two thirds) with social insurance covering a relatively modest 6 per cent of health service spending financed by a payroll tax.

ANNEX 3. TERMS AND DEFINITIONS

The fields of health, social protection and consumer protection all have their own jargons and as the paper slips between them, a glossary of terms is helpful. Many of the following terms are taken from the International Labour Office's recent publications Extending social security to workers in the informal economy: lessons from international experience, ILO 2021, and World Social Protection report, 2020-22. They are sometimes slightly expanded for clarification. ILO Recommendations have been invoked in the preparation of this programme. The glossary is set out in alphabetical order concluding in a distinct list applied to the informal economy. It is preceded by the following list of acronyms, divided into 'families' e.g., WHO.

Cash transfer programme: a non-contributory scheme or programme providing cash benefits to individuals or households, usually financed by taxation, other government revenue or external grants or loans. Cash transfer programmes may or may not include a means test. (See below).

Cash transfer programmes that provide cash to families subject to the condition that they fulfil specific behavioural requirements are often referred to as conditional cash transfer programmes. Such conditions may mean, for example, that beneficiaries must ensure that their children attend school regularly or that they utilize basic preventive nutrition and health-care services.

Contributory scheme: a scheme in which contributions made by protected persons directly determine the entitlement to benefits (acquired rights). The most common type of contributory social security scheme is a statutory social insurance scheme, which usually covers workers in formal wage employment and in some countries also covers the self-employed.

In the case of social insurance schemes for those in waged employment, contributions are usually paid by both employees and employers (though in general, employment injury schemes are fully financed by employers). Contributory schemes may be wholly financed by contributions but are often partly financed by taxation or from other sources; this may be done through a subsidy to cover the deficit or a general subsidy that supplants contributions altogether, or by subsidizing only specific groups of contributors or beneficiaries (e.g. those not contributing because they are caring for children; studying; in military service;

unemployed; or have too low a level of income to fully contribute).

'Force majeure' refers to catastrophes which are unavoidable for individuals and that interrupt the expected course of events, thus preventing participants to a contract from fulfilling obligations. In legal terms the concept may take the form of a clause that is included in contracts to remove liability or suspend obligations. Typical cases in consumer terms would include credit repayment obligations, or rental and/or public utility payments, for which payment holidays have been introduced in many jurisdictions during the COVID-19 pandemic. It has also become associated with governmental declarations of emergencies which may justify such suspensions. (This definition was not developed by ILO).

Means-tested scheme: a scheme that provides benefits upon proof of need and targets certain categories of persons or households whose means fall below a certain threshold, is often referred to as a "social assistance scheme". A means test is used to assess whether the individual's or household's own resources (income and/or assets) are below a defined threshold and to determine whether the applicants are eligible for benefits at all and if so, at what level such benefits will be provided. In some countries, 'proxy' means tests are used: that is, eligibility is determined without directly assessing income or assets but instead based on other household characteristics (proxies) that are deemed more easily observable. Means-tested schemes may also include entitlement conditions and obligations, such as work requirements, participation in health check-ups or (for children) school attendance.

Some means-tested schemes also include other interventions that are delivered on top of the actual income transfer itself. This is sometimes referred to as 'passporting' where, for example, certified entitlement to a means tested benefit may mean automatic entitlement to say free prescription drugs, or free school meals, without a new application having to be made.

Means tests require a 'unit of assessment' that is definition of the family unit entitled to receive financial support. This can raise difficult issues, such as those around ageing populations and multi-generational families with elderly members requiring care. A WHO/

World Bank analysis published in 2021 reports that members of multigenerational households had higher rates than other households of impoverishment due to out-of-pocket health spending.

Non-contributory schemes: includes those benefits in cash or in kind which are means-tested, and those that require no direct contribution from beneficiaries or their employers as a condition of entitlement to receive relevant benefits. The term covers a broad range of schemes, including universal schemes for all residents (such as a national health service); categorical financial support for certain broad groups of the population (e.g., for children under a certain age or older persons over a certain age); and means- tested schemes (such as social assistance schemes or medical services for the poor). Non-contributory schemes are usually financed by taxes or other state revenues, or, in certain cases, external grants or loans.

Out of pocket spending on health (OOPS): WHO, Global spending on health: a world in transition, 2019: Out-of-pocket spending (OOPS) is a payment by households directly to providers to obtain services and health products. It includes purely private transactions (individual payments to private doctors and pharmacies), official patient cost-sharing (user fees / co-payments) within defined public or private benefit packages, and informal payments (payments beyond what is prescribed within benefit entitlements, both in cash and in kind). Thus, OOPS can occur as an explicit part of policy or simply through market transactions, or both.

Social assistance scheme/programme: a scheme that provides benefits to vulnerable groups of the population, especially households living in poverty. Most social assistance schemes are means-tested.

Social insurance (social insurance) scheme: a contributory social protection scheme that guarantees protection through an insurance mechanism, based on: (1) the prior payment of contributions (i.e., before the occurrence of the insured contingency); (2) "risk-sharing" or "pooling"; and (3) the notion of a guarantee. The contributions paid by (or for) insured persons are pooled and the resulting fund is used to cover the expenses incurred exclusively by those persons affected by the occurrence of the relevant (clearly defined) contingency such as sickness. Contrary to commercial insurance, risk-pooling in social insurance is based on the principle of solidarity as opposed to individually calculated risk premiums.

Many contributory social security schemes are presented and described as "insurance" schemes (usually "social insurance schemes") despite being in fact of mixed character, with some non-contributory elements in the entitlement to benefits that allow for a more equitable distribution of benefits, particularly for those with low incomes and short or interrupted work careers. Such non-contributory elements take various forms and are financed either by other contributors (redistribution within the scheme) or the State.

Social protection & social security: In many contexts, the two terms, "social security" and "social protection" may be largely interchangeable, and the ILO certainly uses both in discourse with its constituents. In this report, reference is made to "social protection" both as an alternative expression for "social security" and to denote the protection provided by social security to manage social risks and needs. The SDG report for 2021 distinguishes between health care and cash benefits, the term social protection applying to the latter, including sickness benefits where payable. However, ILO Recommendation 202 (see next item) includes health services as part of social protection.

Social protection floor: ILO Recommendation No. 202 provides that member States should establish and maintain national social protection floors. Such guarantees should ensure at a minimum that, over the life cycle, all in need have access to at least essential health care and basic income security, which together ensure effective access to the essential goods and services defined as necessary at the national level. More specifically, national social protection floors should comprise at least the following four social security guarantees, as defined at the national level:

1. access to essential health care, including maternity care;

2. basic income security for children, providing access to nutrition, education, care, and any other necessary goods and services;

3. basic income security for persons of active age who are unable to earn sufficient income, in particular in cases of sickness, unemployment, maternity and disability;

4. basic income security for older persons.

Social security: the fundamental right to social security is set out in the Universal Declaration of Human Rights of 1948 and other international legal instruments. The notion of social security adopted here covers all measures that provide benefits, whether in cash or in kind, to secure protection, inter alia, from:

1. a lack of work-related income (or insufficient income) caused by sickness, disability, maternity, employment injury, unemployment, old age, or the death of a family member;

2. a lack of (affordable) access to health care;

3. insufficient family support, particularly for children and adult dependants;

4. general poverty and social exclusion.

Social security thus has two key (functional) dimensions, namely "income security" and "availability of medical care", as reflected in the Declaration of Philadelphia of 1944, which forms part of the ILO's Constitution: "social security measures to provide a basic income to all in need of such protection and comprehensive medical care" (III(f)).

Two key features distinguish social security from other social arrangements. First, benefits are provided to beneficiaries without any simultaneous reciprocal obligation (it does not, for example, represent remuneration for work or other services delivered). Second, it is not based on an individual agreement between the protected person and the provider (such as a life insurance contract); the agreement applies to a wider group of people and therefore has a collective character.

Social register: This term has featured in discussion with partners with reference to the need for registration of individuals in the context of entitlement to social protection services such as social insurance and health services and thus to measures of coverage. The extension of social protection beyond social insurance and into the 'informal economies' may be done on a 'rough and ready' approximate basis without strict registration, (for example, by residential zone). However, a more permanent system of entitlement is likely to require a register of entitlement in order to maintain records of associated payments (such as health costs or sickness benefit) in order to avoid abuses such as double claims or criminal activities. Such documentation (which may be digital) is referred to here as social registers. It is closely associated with identity and its proof as an access key to service. This is a working definition, not necessarily endorsed by the United Nations or its constituent bodies such as ILO. Individuals may be listed in more than one social register, for example, one for health service registration and one for social insurance as is commonly the case.

Universal scheme/categorical scheme: strictly speaking, universal schemes provide benefits under the single condition of residence. However, the term is also often used to describe categorical schemes that provide benefits to certain broad categories of the population without a means test or contribution test. The most common forms of such schemes transfer income to older persons over a certain age or children below a certain age. Some categorical schemes also target households with specific structures (one-parent households, for example) or occupational groups (such as rural workers). In some schemes, the entitlement to benefits may be conditional on the performance of specific tasks, or may apply to specific groups in emergencies, such as refugees. Most categorical schemes are tax-financed.

"Informal economy" definitions: It is generally understood that the term "informal economy" covers all economic activities by workers and economic units that are – in law or in practice – not covered or only partially covered by formal arrangements (ILO Recommendation No. 204, para. 2). "Employment in the informal sector": The informal sector is a subset of unincorporated enterprises that are not constituted as separate entities independently of their owners, (and) which typically operate at a low level of organization, on a small scale and with little or no division of labour and capital as factors of production. Typically, "Informal employment" includes those whose employment relationship is, in law or in practice, not subject to national labour legislation income taxation, social protection or entitlement to certain employment benefits. Informal employment may sometimes include informal workers employed in formal enterprises.

Dependants: Definition of dependency is a difficult issue open to diverse cultural and legal interpretations. It may involve, for example, a break point at which young people are treated as adults and thus non-dependant. Many traditions treat married women as dependant on their husbands. Unmarried couples living together may be treated as autonomous individuals, while married couples in similar material circumstances may be treated as a single unit for benefit calculations. Of rising importance as populations live longer, is the care of the elderly or people with disabilities, who may share the family home or may live nearby but may still require regular help and attendance. For purposes of medical records and associated financial records for income support, some WHO colleagues therefore suggest the use of 'family folders'. However, this may require safeguards within folders to maintain confidentiality of medical records.

NOTES

1. United Nations Development Account project on *"Strengthening Social Protection for Pandemic Responses: Identifying the Vulnerable, Aiding Recovery and Building Resilience"*, Cluster I *"Enhanced capacity for social protection"* (Project 2023Y) - https://www.un.org/development/desa/da/wp-content/uploads/sites/52/2020/08/2023Y_Strengthening-Social-Protection-for-Pandemic-Response-.pdf.

2. https://www.un.org/development/desa/da/strengthening-social-protection-for-pandemic-response.

3. Resolution 70/186 on Consumer protection, 22 December 2015 - https://unctad.org/system/files/official-document/ares70d186_en.pdf.

4. https://unctad.org/system/files/official-document/ditccplpmisc2016d1_en.pdf.

5. UNCTAD/DITC/CPLP/2017/2 - https://unctad.org/system/files/official-document/ditccplp2017d2_en.pdf.

6. For example, the presentation of Nievia Ramsundar, Executive Director the Caribbean Community (CARICOM), Competition Commission, *Regional response of the Caribbean to consumer concerns during the pandemic,* to the regional webinar *"Consumer Protection and health during Covid-19: experiences from Latin America and the Caribbean"* 12/03/21 convened by the Pan-American Health Organization (PAHO) and UNCTAD: *"The pandemic has shown that the provision of health services is no less a consumer matter than any other".*

7. *Declaration of ministers of the least developed countries at the 15th session.* UNCTAD, Barbados, 2021 para d)

8. Ms. Amina Mohammed, Deputy Secretary-General, United Nations, plenary session, UNCTAD 15.

9. See Annex 1 Recommendations 2,3,7,8 and 9. In the analysis that follows, the Phase 1 recommendations, which are all set out in Annex 1, are referred to by the titles rather than by numbers, to avoid confusion with recommendations emanating from this Phase 3 report.

10. The third refers to measures to maintain incomes during pandemics. See Annex 1

11. The global indicator list is contained in the *Report of the Inter-Agency and Expert Group on Sustainable Development Goal Indicators (E/CN.3/2016/2/Rev.1), Annex IV.*

12. ILO, *Social Protection Spotlight:* January 2020. *Towards universal health coverage: social health protection principles.* P.2 further reference to ILO 2008, *Social Health Protection: An ILO strategy towards universal access to health care.*

13. *Global monitoring report on financial protection in health* 2021. WHO, World Bank 2021. WHO Global *spending on health: a world in transition,* WHO, 2019 see critique of social insurance p.51.

14. See Annex 3 on definitions. See also ILO *Extending social security to workers in the informal economy: lessons from international experience.* 2021 and *World Social Protection report 2020-22.*

15. UNGA Resolution 2200A (XXI) of 16 December 1966.

16. *Constitution of the World Health Organisation*, the Constitution was adopted by the International Health Conference held in New York from 19 June to 22 July 1946, signed on 22 July 1946.

17. ILO Spotlight *op cit,* pp 3&4. ILO Recommendation 202. *Social Protection Floors*, 2012. Para 5.8 a).

18. Global indicator framework *op cit.* 2021 revision.

19. United Nations Sustainable Development Goals Report 2021, p.10 & 27. See also, United Nations Committee for the Coordination of Statistical Activities (CCSA), *Social impact, How COVID-19 is changing the world: a statistical perspective,* p.44. CCSA distinguishes social protection from health services.

20. United Nations Sustainable Development Goals Report 2021, p.33. It is important to note that although the Index runs from 1 to 100, it does not represent the percentages of population, estimated to have access.

21. WHO SEARO, *'Crisis or opportunity, Health finance in times of uncertainty: country profiles for the SEA region.* p.3, note a) *2021.*

22. WHO, World Bank, Global *monitoring report on financial protection in health* 2021. Executive summary.

23. WHO (2016). *Global diffusion of eHealth: Making universal health coverage achievable*, Report of third global survey of ehealth. Global observatory for ehealth, WHO 2016.

24. UNDP Sustainable *Development Goals report 2021.* P.27

25. Gentilini *et al,* Social *Protection and Jobs Responses to COVID-19: A Real-Time Review of Country Measures* "Living paper" version 15 (May 2021) World Bank p. 5 & Table 1.

26. (African) *Regional Dialogue on the role of consumer protection and social protection in the post COVID recovery in the provision of health services including e-health*, 27 April 2021. Ms. Karima Ben Soltane, Director of the Institute for Development and Economic Planning, ECA, *Talking Points.*

27. Gentilini *et al* 2021, *op cit.* p. 4 & p.5 Fig 2.

28. Gentilini *et al. Op cit.*p.7 & Table 5.

29. Gentilini *et al op cit.* p. 6 & Tables 3 & 4. Utility payment postponement was greatly outnumbered by labour market programmes such as wage subsidy, working hours, training, and labour regulation measures 806 measures in 178 countries by May 2021. The report describes the rate of adoption of such measures as 'resounding'.

30 Covid19 Consumer Law Research Group, *Consumer Law and Policy Relating to Change of Circumstances Due to the COVID-19 Pandemic,* Journal of Consumer Policy 43.03/08/202.

31 UNDP, The Sustainable Development Goals Report 2020. SDG 16, p.58

32 OECD, IOM (International Organisation on Migration), ILO, UNHCR (High Commission on Refugees), 2020 *Annual International migration and forced displacement trends and policies report to the G20.* 2020. P.3

33 United Nations, Resolution adopted by the General Assembly on 19 September 2016, 71/1. *New York Declaration for Refugees and Migrants* para eighty-three

34 Notification from WHO EMRO, 2022.

35 Confirmed in correspondence by WHO EMRO,

36 WHO. *Promoting the health of refugees and migrants: draft global action plan, 2019–2023.* 2019. Our thanks to WHO EMRO for this information, including 2nd draft of strategy (unpublished yet). 'Mainstreaming' is discussed as a way of integrating refugees and migrants into national health policies and plans. WHO discussions (e.g., WHO EMRO *Refugee & migrant health strategy – consultation meeting* 07/07/21) have also taken in reducing tensions between refugees/migrants and host communities in this context.

37 Source: G20 Digital Identity Onboarding Report, see Phase 1 report.

38 Magdalena Sepúlveda Carmona, *Is biometric technology in social protection programmes illegal or arbitrary? An analysis of privacy and data protection* Social Protection Department, ILO Geneva, ESS – Extension of Social Security Working Paper No. 59, 2018. p 14

39 Turkish Red Crescent and World Food Programme, 2019, *Refugees in Turkey: Livelihood Survey Findings,* accessed March 2021.

40 R. Peconga & H Thogersen, *Post-traumatic stress disorder, depression, and anxiety in adult Syrian refugees: What do we know?* Scandinavian Journal of Public Health, 48(7), 2019.

41 D Statis G20 in figures, summit of the G20 states in Hamburg, 2017. Federal statistical office of Germany.

42 OECD, IOM, ILO, UNHCR, 2020 *op cit.*

43 Syrian Arab Republic, the Bolivarian Republic of Venezuela, Afghanistan, South Sudan, Myanmar, UNHCR *Global Trends 2020.*

44 UNHCR, *Global compact on refugees* United Nations 2018. Programme of Action, paras 58 and 82.

45 UNHCR: *Global compact on refugees:* indicator framework, United Nations 2019. Annex 2.

46 Refugees are a particular category of migrants with rights derived under relevant international conventions on refugee status. However, not all refugees are granted refugee status and may be referred to as migrants. Our thanks to WHO EMRO for this explanation.

47 Robert Holzmann and Wels Jacques' 2019 Austrian Academy of Sciences, University of New South Wales, University of Cambridge and Université libre de Bruxelles.

48 African Union Commission (2021). *Draft AU Interoperability Framework for Digital ID* (August 2021).

49 ILO C. 102. Social Security (Minimum Standards) Convention, 1952 ILO home, accessed 25/11/21. ILO ROAF *Extending social protection to migrant workers in the ECOWAS region.: a capacity building toolkit on the ECOWAS general convention on social security. Social protection for migrant workers: an overview.* Module 2 July 2019.

50 United Nations, *Global compact for safe, orderly and regular migration,* adopted 11 12/2018.paras 22 & 38.

51 United Nations General Assembly, Resolution 70/186 Consumer protection. 22/12/2015. Guidelines 5 & 3.

52 UNCTAD, *Access by consumers to essential services, energy water and sanitation.* United Nations 2022. p18 and other.

53 UNCTAD (2017) *Manual on Consumer Protection*, V Foster & C. Briceno-Garmendia, *Africa's infrastructure: a time for Transformation, summary of main findings.* World Bank, 2010. p.14. Andres et al. *Doing more with less: Smarter Subsidies for Water Supply and Sanitation*, Overview, World Bank, 2019, xv.

54 D Mitlin & D Satterthwaite, *Urban poverty in the global South: scale and nature.* 2013. pp.89, 104 & 296

55 UNCTAD, Achieving the SDGs through consumer protection, United Nations 2017 chapter iv.

56 Jim Yong Kim, WBG, *Financial Times,* October 17, 2014. *There is a strong economic case for universal health coverage.*

57 The WHO health expenditure report 2019 defines OOPS as follows: "Out-of-pocket spending is a payment by households directly to providers to obtain services and health products. It includes purely private transactions (individual payments to private doctors and pharmacies), official patient cost-sharing (user fees / co-payments) within defined public or private benefit packages, and informal payments (payments beyond what is prescribed within benefit entitlements, both in cash and in kind). Thus, OOPS can occur as an explicit part of policy or simply through market transactions, or both". Discussed in Annex 2

58 Global monitoring report on financial protection in health 2021. WHO, World Bank 2021 P. ix.

59 ILO, *Social Protection Spotlight:* January 2020. P. 3

60 WHO, *Global spending on health: a world in transition,* WHO, 2019, Box 1.1

61 ILO, *Social Protection Spotlight:* January 2020. *Op cit.*

62 United Nations *SDG Report 2020*, SDG 3 *Good health & wellbeing*, p. 31

63 *Global monitoring report on financial protection in health* 2021. WHO, World Bank 2021 Exec summary

64 *SDG 3 tracker* SDG indicator 3.8.2 accessed March 2022

65 WHO/World Bank: *Global monitoring report on financial protection in health.* 2021. Exec summary.

66 WHO SEARO 2021 *op cit.* p. 63ff.

67 WHO SEARO 2021 *op cit.* p. 63ff. See Annex 2.

68 WHO SEARO 2021 *op cit.* p. 75ff.

69 WHO SEARO Figs 9, 10 & 11b.

70 WHO SEARO2021 *op cit.* p. 10

71 WHO SEARO 2021, *op cit.* fig 11b

72 Hui Wang et al, *financial protection analysis in eight countries in the WHO South-East Asia Region* World Health Organization Regional Office for South-East Asia, *Bull World Health Organ* 2018, Bangladesh, Bhutan India, Maldives, Nepal, Sri Lanka, Thailand, and Timor-Leste. Table 5.

73 WHO, Global *spending on health: weathering the storm*, 2020 pp 49 & 73.

74 WHO *Global spending on health: weathering the storm*, 2020 p. 76

75 WHO SEARO 2021 *op cit. Recommendations.*

76 WHO SEARO 2021, *op cit.* pp 7,10, 18, Fig 11b)

77 UNCTAD *The least-developed countries in a post-COVID world: learning from 50 years of experience.* Relevant SDG targets 1.3 (social protection) and 3.8 (health). Table 4.2 p. 104.

78 WHO, *Public spending on health: a closer look at global trends,* 2018. p. 26 and Fig 3.5

79 H. Wang et al. *financial protection analysis in eight countries in the WHO South-East Asia Region* WHO SEARO *Bull World Health Organ* 2018 Bangladesh, Bhutan, India, Maldives, Nepal, Sri Lanka, Thailand, and Timor-Leste.

80 UNCTAD, *Manual on Consumer Protection*, ch 17, 2016; also *Achieving the SDGs through consumer protection* ch 4, 2017.

81 WHO / WBG survey: *Global monitoring report on financial protection in health in 2019.* WHO and World Bank Group (2020), p. 12/13

82 WHO (2019). *Global spending on health: a world in transition,* WHO, 2019 p. 40.

83 WHO (2019) *Global spending on health: a world in transition,* Fig 4.7

84 *Medicines reimbursement policies in Europe.* WHO Europe 2018. P. xiii

85 OECD, *Health at a Glance 2019: OECD Indicators.* The dates for the estimates are around 2017 and the same table features in the 2020 edition.

86 H Wang et al, *op cit.* p. 614.

87 See Annex 3 for definition of social registers. Their expansion is discussed in Section 5.2

88 The full title of SDG 16 is: *Promote peaceful and inclusive societies for sustainable development, provide access to justice for all and build effective, accountable, and inclusive institutions at all levels*

89 UNDP The Sustainable Development Goals Report 2020. P. 56. The relevant indicator 16.9.1 is *"Proportion of children under 5 years of age whose births have been registered with a civil authority"* Global indicator framework for the Sustainable Development Goals and targets of the 2030 Agenda for Sustainable Development SDG 16, p. 19/22

90 UNDP SDG Report 2021 p. 5

91 UNCTAD, Cote d'Ivoire, *Evaluation de l'état de préparation au commerce électronique.* Pp 1 & 67.

92 ID4D (2018) *Data Note - ID4D Global Dataset and ID4D-Findex Survey.* Cited in A. Van der Spuy, V. Bandari, S. Trikanad, Y Tshering Paul. *Towards the evaluation of socio-digital ID ecosystems in Africa: comparative analysis of findings from 10 country case studies.* Research ICT Africa, the centre for the Internet & Society, Omidyar Network. November 2021. p. 10

93 K. Lindert, T.G. Karippacheril, I. Rodriguez Caillava & K. Nishikawa Chavez. *Sourcebook on the Foundations of Social Protection delivery systems,* World Bank 2020 p. 29

94 Dakar AMREF conference 1/12/21 *Achime Malik N'Diaye, Minister of Digital Economy, Senegal,*

95 UNICEF/World Bank: Common Ground: UNICEF and World Bank *Approaches to Building Social Protection Systems* 2013.p.2

96 UNICEF/World Bank: Common Ground: UNICEF and World Bank *Approaches to Building Social Protection Systems* 2013. p. 2 Similar doubts including the dangers of 'mass surveillance' have been expressed by the United Nations as noted in the Phase 1 report.

97 Magdalena Sepúlveda Carmona, United Nations Research Institute for Social Development, **International** *Social Security Review,* Vol. 72, 4/2019 *Biometric technology and beneficiary rights in social protection programmes. p. 4.*

[98] The Indian Supreme Court ruled in 2017 that enrolment in Aadhaar, the identity system based on biometric identifiers which is used for entitlement for public services, should not be mandatory for access to services. Supreme Court of India. Case of Justice KS. *Puttaswamy (Retd.)* vs. *Union of India and Others*, 24 August 2017.

[99] A. Van der Spuy, V. Bandari, S. Trikanad, Y Tshering Paul. *Towards the evaluation of socio-digital ID ecosystems in Africa: comparative analysis of findings from 10 country case studies.* Research ICT Africa, the centre for the Internet & Society, Omidyar Network. November 2021. Executive summary & p. 57

[100] , K. Lindert, *et al* World Bank, 2020.*op cit.* p. 92/3

[101] WHO (2016). *Global diffusion of eHealth: Making universal health coverage achievable,* Report of third global survey of ehealth. Global observatory for ehealth, WHO 2016.

[102] ITU/UNESCO Broadband Commission for sustainable development, *the state of broadband 2021: people centred approaches for universal broadband.* September 2021. P. xiii & p.6-7. Source: ITU, 2020 Facts and Figures Measuring Digital Development.

[103] African Union Commission Draft *AU Interoperability Framework for digital ID,* 2021. See also Van der Spuy *et al, op cit.* 2021. P.11

[104] Van der Spuy et al, *op cit.* p. 24/25.

[105] P Burnel, J Mejane, A Rouzier Deroubaix, *Garantir un numérique inclusif : les réponses apportées par les opérateurs de la protection sociale.* Inspection générale des affaires sociales, Décembre 2019, Rapport IGAS 2019-033R

[106] Rapport du défenseur des droits, (English version) Dematerialisation of public services : 3 years later, where are we ? 16/2/22. Republique Française.

[107] M. Sepulveda Carmona, *Is biometric technology in social protection programmes illegal or arbitrary? An analysis of privacy and data protection.* Extension of social security working paper 59. Social protection department, ILO 2018.

[108] WHO Africa RO *Survey on use of digital health services in WHO Africa region,* (ongoing 2022): p. 33

[109] N Archer, C Lokker, M Ghasemaghaei, D DiLeberto. Journal of Medical Internet Research, Vol 23. 18/06/21, eHealth Implementation Issues in Low-Resource Countries: Model, Survey, and Analysis of User Experience, they cite: Hoque MR, Bao Y, Sorwar G. Investigating factors influencing the adoption of e-Health in developing countries: a patient's perspective. Inform Health Soc Care 2017; also: Zayyad M, Toycan M. Factors affecting sustainable adoption of e-health technology in developing countries: an exploratory survey of Nigerian hospitals from the perspective of healthcare professionals. PeerJ 2018

[110] WHO AFRO Covid19 response strategy, May 2020.

[111] See UNCTAD *Access by consumers to essential services, energy water and sanitation.* United Nations 2022, p. 11

[112] UNCTAD, *Manual for consumer protection.* Ch XIII *Privacy and data protection.* United Nations 2017.

[113] Tony Blair Institute for global change, *Digital identity: where are we and where are we going? 14/8/20,* A Bennett, M Beverton-Palmer.

[114] Global indicator framework for the Sustainable Development Goals and targets of the 2030 Agenda for Sustainable Development, most recent revision 2021.

[115] CCSA, *Social impact, How COVID-19 is changing the world: a statistical perspective,* p. 44.

[116] ILO Social protection spotlight: *Towards universal health coverage: social health protection principles. 2020.* Box 2.

[117] D McIntyre & J Kutzin, *Health financing country diagnostic: a foundation for national strategy development.* (Health Financing Guidance No. 1). WHO 2016.

[118] According to F. Bonnet & V. Leung, *Women & men in the informal economy: a statistical picture.* Third edition, ILO, 2018. More than 60 per cent of the world's employed population are in the informal economy. ILO press release, 30/4/18. This adds up to two billion people, 86 per cent of African workers. The percentage drops to half when agriculture is excluded as 90 per cent of this large sector are 'informal'.

[119] ECLAC *Social Panorama of Latin America 2021,* ECLAC 2022. See also *The relationship between Social Protection and Health in Latin America during COVID-19,* Ms. María Luisa Marinho, Oficial Adjunta de Asuntos Sociales de la División de Desarrollo Social/ Social Affairs Officer, Division on Social Development, United Nations Economic Commission for Latin America, and the Caribbean (ECLAC) UNCTAD online seminar 12/03/21.

[120] ECLAC, *Social Panorama of Latin America.* 2021. ECLAC 2022. *op cit.* Our thanks to ECLAC colleagues for updates.

[121] Novissi.gouv.tg intervention in *Rencontres de la santé numérique en Afrique de l'Ouest* 01/12/21. Dakar

[122] Noppakun Thammatacharee et al *Prevalence and profiles of unmet healthcare need in Thailand* BMC Public health 2012 12. WHO SEARO fig 11b

[123] WHO SEARO, 2021, *op cit.* pp. 78 & 125.

[124] B.C. James & G.P. Poulsen, *The case for capitation.* In *Business & Society,* July/August 2016. T. Torrey *How health care capitation payment systems work.* Verywell health 20/02/20. GOV.UK *Capitation, an introduction.* accessed May 2022.

[125] WHO Service delivery & safety, *People-centred & integrated health services: an overview of the evidence.*2015, pp 30 & 35.

[126] Resolution World Health Assembly 58.28, 2005.

[127] WHO Africa region, *"Survey on use of digital health services in WHO Africa region*, (ongoing 2022): *'mHealth is the use of mobile devices, such as mobile phones, patient monitoring devices, Personal Digital Assistants (PDAs), and wireless devices, for medical and public health practice"*. This includes *"treatment adherence, community mobilisation, collecting community and clinical health data, wellness and self-care, chronic disease management, and remote patient monitoring"*. It contributes to public health and *"universal health coverage through making services available to remote populations and underserved communities and providing mechanisms for data exchange on patients"*.

[128] World Health Organisation, 2021, Global strategy on digital health, 2020-2025.glossary.

[129] PAHO/WHO, 2021 *Connectivity & Bandwidth: Key areas for improving public health.* Digital transformation toolkit. Knowledge tools. 2-4. Precisely the same point was made at the recent online seminar of AMREF in Senegal by *Mme Kardiata Sow (TechCare4All – Afrique Francophone). Rencontres de la santé numérique en Afrique de l'Ouest* 01/12/21. Dakar

[130] Our thanks to Liz Coll for this suggestion.

[131] WHO Niger, *Appui technique pour la mise en œuvre des activités du Plan d'Action National d'investissement dans les emplois du secteur sanitaire et social et la croissance économique au Niger* Rapport final de mission, (2020/21) p. 7

[132] AMREF, *Rencontres de la santé numérique en Afrique de l'Ouest* December 1 & 2, 2021. Dakar *Sandrine Busière. (Terre des Hommes – Sénégal)* intervention : *'Les Mamans demandent leurs tablettes'*

[133] Magdalena Sepúlveda Carmona, United Nations Research Institute for Social Development, **International** *Social Security Review,* Vol. 72, 4/2019 *Biometric technology and beneficiary rights in social protection programmes.* UNCTAD, Cote d'Ivoire, *Evaluation de l'état de préparation au commerce électronique.*

[134] See UNCTAD, Cote d'Ivoire, *Evaluation de l'état de préparation au commerce électronique.* 2021.

[135] For further discussion see UNCTAD *Digital economy report, 2021.* United Nations 2021. See presentation by Torbjorn Fredriksson Head, e-commerce and digital economy branch, online seminar: *Making digital markets work for consumers*, 5/11/21: *Cross-border data flows and development: for whom the data flow.*

[136] UNCTAD online seminar 28/03/22 Dr Tayag, Philippines ministry of Health

[137] Z Obermeyer *et al, dissecting racial bias in an algorithm used to manage the health of populations. Science 447,* 2019. Cited in R. Slaughter, *Algorithms & economic justice: a taxonomy of harms and a path forward for the FTC. Yale Journal of Law & Technology,* August 2021. P.16

[138] PAHO/WHO, 2021 *Connectivity & Bandwidth: Key areas for improving public health.* Digital transformation toolkit. Knowledge tools. 2-4. See also *The Lancet* 27/02/1971, 'J. Tudor Hart, *The inverse care law.* Recently revisited in *The Lancet* 27/02/2021: S.W. Mercer, J. Patterson, J.P. Robson, S.M. Smith, E. Walton G. Watt. *The inverse care law & the potential of primary care in deprived areas.*

[139] World Bank (2021) World Development Report 2021, *Data for better lives,* P. 160-167

[140] There is evidence that internet-based platforms and Apps are taking off in low-income countries but restricted to the better off, initially using e-commerce platforms, for example. See UNCTAD e-commerce readiness assessments.

[141] UNCTAD, Cote d'Ivoire, *Evaluation de l'état de préparation au commerce électronique.* Pp 1,2 & 67.

[142] AMREF, 2021, *Rencontres de la santé numérique en Afrique de l'Ouest* 01/12/21. In partnership with WHO and the West African Economic & Monetary Union. Dakar Intervention by Dr Marie Sarr.

[143] Carlos Iglesias, *the gender gap in internet access: using a woman-centred method.* WWW Foundation, 20/03/20. Analysis based on data from The Economist intelligence Unit.

[144] World Bank 2021 *World Development Report op cit* p. 168

[145] This point has been brought to our attention by WHO Africa.

[146] World Bank 2021 *World Development Report op cit.* p. 170

[147] UNCTAD *Digital economy report, 2021.* United Nations 2021. See the UNCTAD Competition and Consumer Policies Branch Webinar *Making digital markets work for consumers*, 5/11/21: *Cross-border data flows and development: for whom the data flow, 2021,* namely the presentation by Torbjorn Fredriksson, UNCTAD, Head, E-commerce and digital economy branch and the reference to the 'need to enable global data-sharing and develop global digital public goods.

[148] See *The Economist,* 'Seeding the cloud' December 4th, 2021, regarding internet investment in Africa.

[149] WHO AFRO survey 2022 *op cit* p. 42.

[150] Prof. Marie-Collette Kamwe Mouaffo, Université de Ngaoundere, Cameroun, online seminar record.

[151] World Bank, *World Development Report 2021, Data for better lives,* p. 157 & 176. WB also called for a *'rethink (of) universal service policies.*

[152] GSMA, *Successful spectrum auctions are key to high quality connectivity.* 09/09/21

[153] ITU/UNESCO Broadband Commission for sustainable development. *The state of broadband 2021: people centred approaches for universal broadband.* 2021 p. 27.

[154] ITU/UNESCO 2021 *op cit.* p. 30

155 International Telecommunications Union, ITU Study Group 1. Paper submitted by Association for Progressive Communications (APC), *The Role of Community Networks as a response to the COVID-19 pandemic*. September 2020.

156 Public Private Infrastructure Advisory Service (World Bank) studies around the turn of the millennium.

157 As widely reported during the five regional webinars during Phase 2 of this project.

158 Long term infrastructure investors association, (2021) *Social infrastructure: from challenge to opportunity for investors*. Pp. 5, 32 and 52/53.

159 WHO Service delivery & safety, *People-centred & integrated health services: an overview of the evidence.*2015, p. 30.

160 UNCTAD Cote d'Ivoire *op cit.* p.22.

161 UNCTAD online seminar 28/03/22with Ministry of Health and Department of Trade & Industry.

162 WHO Africa region survey 2022 *op cit.* p.8

163 WHO Strategy 2020-25 p. 26 see also May 2018 declaration calling for: *"accelerating the development and adoption of appropriate, accessible, affordable, scalable and sustainable person-centric digital health solutions".* WHO Digital Health. 2018 May 26. 4 p. Seventy-First World Health Assembly WHA71.7

164 SDG 1 *End poverty in all its forms everywhere* Target 1.3: *Implement nationally appropriate social protection systems and measures for all, including floors.* SDG 3: *Ensure healthy lives and promote well-being for all at all ages.* Target 3.8: *Achieve universal health coverage, including financial risk protection, access to quality essential health-care services and access to safe, effective, quality, and affordable essential medicines and vaccines for all.*

165 United Nations Sustainable Development Goals Report 2021. P.27 U. Gentilini *et al*, Social *Protection and Jobs Responses to COVID-19: A Real-Time Review of Country Measures* "Living paper" version 15 (May 2021) World Bank p. 5 & Table 1.

166 United Nations, Resolution adopted by the General Assembly on 19 September 2016, 71/1. *New York Declaration for Refugees and Migrants* para 83

167 United Nations, *global compact for safe, orderly and regular migration,* adopted 11 12/2018.para 22 & 38.

168 D. Mitlin & D Satterthwaite, *Urban poverty in the global South: scale and nature.* 2013. pp.89, 104 & 296D

169 WHO/World Bank: *Global monitoring report on financial protection in health.* 2021. Exec summary.

170 ILO recommendation 202 Social protection floors: Article 5.8 (a) *persons in need of health care should not face hardship and an increased risk of poverty due to the financial consequences of accessing essential health care. Free prenatal and postnatal medical care for the most vulnerable should also be considered;* ILO Social protection Spotlight January 2020.

171 https://www.who.int/health_financing/UHCandHealthFinancing-final.pdf. Accessed March 2022

172 For discussion of equity see D. McIntyre & J. Kutzin, Health *financing country diagnostic: a foundation for national strategy development.* Health financing guidance 1. WHO 2016.

173 [add publication number and classification]